The Rabbi's Magic Trick

More Kosher Bridge

David Bird, the world's leading humorous bridge writer, joins forces again with Ron Klinger, one of the world's best-known bridge teachers and authors. The result is a scintillating new collection of stories about the bridge-playing Rabbi.

Where else would you find an unnervingly plausible account of a Rabbi gambling his holiday money in a high-stake rubber game against three wealthy Arabs? And where might you chance upon a parable such as the Synagogue team facing a team of Catholic priests and nuns (hired professionals!) as part of the St Benedict Commemoration celebrations?

As readers of *Kosher Bridge* and *Kosher Bridge 2* will expect, the humour is sparkling and the bridge brilliant. Sit back, hold tight, and enjoy this vastly entertaining book.

The Rabbi's Magic Trick

More Kosher Bridge

David Bird & Ron Klinger

VICTOR GOLLANCZ
in association with
PETER CRAWLEY

First published in Great Britain 1998
in association with Peter Crawley
by Victor Gollancz
An imprint of the Cassell Group
Wellington House, 125 Strand, London WC2R 0BB

A catalogue record for this book
is available from the British Library

ISBN 0 575 06595 8

Photoset in Great Britain by
Rowland Phototypesetting Ltd, Bury St Edmunds
and printed by St Edmundsbury Press Ltd,
Bury St Edmunds, Suffolk

Contents

1.   The Cantor's Hot Streak

'The room looks good, yes?' queried Miriam.

The Cantor sighed. 'It looked good last time you asked me,' he replied. 'Five minutes later it still looks good.'

'Well, that Judith has eyes like a hawk,' declared Miriam. 'If anything is not quite right, she will notice.'

'It's just as well men aren't like that,' observed the Cantor. 'You think when we play bridge at their place I go looking for some surface that has not been dusted?'

'You would not find one, believe me,' replied Miriam. 'Not at Judith's place when she has visitors. I have looked.'

The door bell rang. 'Ah, they are on time for a change,' said Miriam, checking her hair in the hall mirror. 'You have the wine ready, Michael, and the new crystal glasses?'

'Yes, yes,' replied Cantor. 'And I have checked that they have no speck of dust on them.'

'Don't be silly,' said Miriam. 'Open the door for them, will you? You think it will open itself?'

Judith and her husband, Maurice, were admitted and the four made their way into the sitting room. 'How is business, Maurice?' asked the Cantor, as they took their places around the card table.

'Ah, not so good, not so bad,' replied the silver-haired Maurice.

'The cash flow?' continued the Cantor. 'You were worried about it last time we spoke.'

Maurice's face darkened. 'So many people pay me late nowadays, it is a disgrace,' he declared. 'If I didn't make my own payments even later I would be in trouble, believe me.'

'Stop talking business, Michael,' reprimanded Miriam. 'You know Judith and I can't stand it.'

Play began and this was the first hand:

Love all   ♠ A 10 7 3
Dealer North   ♡ –
                              ◇ A K J 7 6
                              ♣ 9 8 6 3

♠ K 2   ♠ Q J 8
♡ A 10 8 6 3   **N**   ♡ K Q 9 4 2
◇ 5   **W   E**   ◇ 10 9 4 3
♣ K Q J 10 2   **S**   ♣ 4

                              ♠ 9 6 5 4
                              ♡ J 7 5
                              ◇ Q 8 2
                              ♣ A 7 5

West	*North*	*East*	*South*
Judith	Miriam	Maurice	The Cantor
–	1◇	Pass	1♠
2NT	4♠	All Pass	

Judith, whose black hair was tied in an elegant bun, intervened with 2NT. This was the Unusual No-trump, showing the two unbid suits. Realising that the opponents had a big heart fit, Miriam jumped to Four Spades in the hope that this would shut Maurice out of the auction. There was no further bidding and Judith led the king of clubs.

The Cantor won the club lead with the ace and played a trump to dummy's 10 and East's jack. The king of hearts return was ruffed in the dummy and the Cantor cashed the ace of trumps, both defenders following. The rest of the hand was easy. He cashed the five diamond winners, discarding two clubs, and cross-ruffed in hearts and clubs. East could score his queen of trumps whenever he wished. It would be the third and last trick for the defence.

Judith's mouth dropped. 'You had five hearts, Maurice?' she gasped.

'I don't recall,' replied her husband. 'Four or five hearts, yes.'

'Why didn't you bid after my 2NT?' persisted Judith. 'Four Spades they make here and Five Hearts is only one down.'

'You don't read Eddie Schlussel's column in the Jewish Times?' countered Maurice. '*"The five level is for the opponents"*. Only last week he wrote it.'

Miriam sat happily in her chair. Judith and Maurice were arguing already and Michael had actually played a hand properly for a change. Perhaps she was dreaming. Even better, it seemed that Judith might have missed a chance in the defence.

Miriam turned towards Judith. 'What happens if you put in the king of trumps on the first round?' she said. 'Michael must win or you will cash two clubs. Now if he plays another trump Maurice will win and play a third round. Michael would then be one trick short.'

Maurice nodded fervently. 'Yes, I would play a third round,' he said. 'You see, Judith? I would win the second round with the jack and straight away play the queen.'

Judith blinked. 'Don't be ridiculous,' she declared. 'If I put in the king of trumps and declarer holds something like Q 9 x x he would pick up the suit for no losers.'

Maurice was not listening. 'That man Schlussel knows what he is talking about,' he said, tapping the side of his nose. 'You don't go wandering up to the five level when the opponents' game should go one down.'

'Should go down, he says,' exclaimed Judith. 'What rubbish you talk, Maurice.'

Maurice turned to the Cantor. 'You know the definition of a Jewish husband, Michael?'

'So, tell me.'

'A man who gives his wife the best ears of his life,' said Maurice, looking pleased with himself.

'Good, yes,' replied the Cantor. 'Or, perhaps it could be: a man of few words.'

The score soon reached Game All, then the Cantor had a chance to win the rubber.

Game all
Dealer South

```
                    ♠ J 6
                    ♡ A 8 5 4
                    ◇ K 6 2
                    ♣ J 10 6 2
    ♠ Q 10 8 2                      ♠ A 9 5 3
    ♡ 9 7 3 2         N            ♡ J 10 6
    ◇ 10 9 5 3    W       E         ◇ J 7
    ♣ 9              S             ♣ K Q 8 7
                    ♠ K 7 4
                    ♡ K Q
                    ◇ A Q 8 4
                    ♣ A 5 4 3
```

West	North	East	South
Judith	*Miriam*	*Maurice*	*The Cantor*
–	–	–	1♣
Pass	1♡	Pass	2NT
Pass	3NT	All Pass	

Not overimpressed by the sight of only 2 points in her hand, Judith led a low spade against 3NT. Maurice captured dummy's jack with the ace and returned ♠3, won by Judith's 8. The Cantor won the third round of spades and paused to count his tricks. Three hearts, three diamonds, and two winners in the black suits. The spades seemed to be 4–4, so there was no hurry to look for a 3–3 break in the diamond suit.

The Cantor cashed the king and queen of hearts, then led a low club from his hand. Maurice won dummy's jack with the queen and returned a spade to West's 10, declarer throwing a club from both hands. Judith's diamond switch went to the jack and declarer's queen. The Cantor was on lead in this end position:

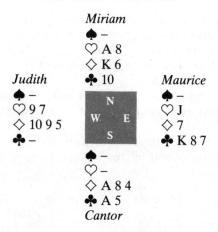

Miriam
♠ –
♡ A 8
◇ K 6
♣ 10

Judith
♠ –
♡ 9 7
◇ 10 9 5
♣ –

Maurice
♠ –
♡ J
◇ 7
♣ K 8 7

♠ –
♡ –
◇ A 8 4
♣ A 5
Cantor

When the ace of clubs was played Judith had no good discard. Following the sound maxim of guarding against the threat she could actually see, she kept her hearts and threw a diamond. The Cantor now cashed the heart ace and three diamond tricks to make the game.

'How can you do this to me, Maurice?' exclaimed Judith.

'Me?' her husband replied. 'You throw a diamond and for some reason it is my fault?'

'Throw a diamond, throw a heart, it makes no difference,' declared Judith. 'What I would like to throw is a spade.'

Maurice looked back uncomprehendingly. 'There were no spades left,' he said.

'I had no spade left because you removed it yourself,' persisted Judith. 'Come off lead with a heart and she cannot make it. If she cashes the ace of clubs I can throw the spade.'

This was too much for Maurice. 'Next time if you don't want to cash a long spade, don't bother setting it up,' he said.

'I make the rubber 13 points,' declared Miriam. 'You have the wine ready, Michael?'

'Ah yes, excellent,' exclaimed Maurice, as he took his first sip of the well-chilled Yarden Chardonnay. 'You get this from David Eltzinger?'

'I do, but I shouldn't,' replied the Cantor. 'What a merchant he is. Can you believe he charges £8.99 for this?'

'Cheaper everywhere else, I know,' replied Maurice. 'But times are hard for them. His son, Ronnie, and that pretty young Mitzi, they are both still at college.'

'Of course, that's why I buy from him,' replied the Cantor. 'Once they have graduated I will go to the supermarket instead, believe me.'

Play restarted and both sides scored an early game. Once more a chance to win the rubber fell to the Cantor.

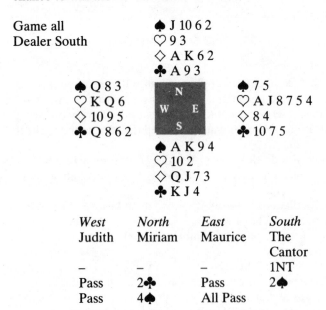

Game all   ♠ J 10 6 2
Dealer South   ♡ 9 3
                ♢ A K 6 2
                ♣ A 9 3

♠ Q 8 3   ♠ 7 5
♡ K Q 6   ♡ A J 8 7 5 4
♢ 10 9 5   ♢ 8 4
♣ Q 8 6 2   ♣ 10 7 5

                ♠ A K 9 4
                ♡ 10 2
                ♢ Q J 7 3
                ♣ K J 4

West	*North*	*East*	*South*
Judith	Miriam	Maurice	The Cantor
–	–	–	1NT
Pass	2♣	Pass	2♠
Pass	4♠	All Pass	

Judith led the king of hearts against Four Spades, continuing with the queen when she received an encouraging signal. At trick 3 she switched to ♢10. The Cantor won with dummy's ace and played the jack of trumps. When a low card appeared from East he paused for thought. If West didn't hold the club queen, she might well have switched to clubs rather than diamonds. And if there was a loser in the club suit it was important to get the trumps right. Could Maurice hold the trump queen? No, he was a life-long follower of the 'cover an honour with an honour' rule. It must be better to try to drop the queen from Judith's hand.

The Cantor overtook the jack of trumps with the ace and drew a second round with the king. No joy came from this, the queen refusing to show. Four rounds of diamonds followed, West discarding a club on the fourth round. Ah well, thought the Cantor, it would have to be the club finesse. Unless . . . wait a minute! What if he played a trump now? Judith would perhaps have nothing safe to play back.

Judith was less than pleased to see a trump appear on the table. She won with the queen and exited with the queen of clubs, hoping to put declarer to a guess if he held A 10 x in the suit.

'They're all there now,' said the Cantor, facing his remaining cards.

Miriam could scarcely believe her eyes. 'I have never seen you play so well, Michael,' she said. 'Why couldn't you play like this on Tuesday night?'

'It was an easy hand,' replied the Cantor. 'When Maurice didn't cover in trumps I knew Judith must hold the queen.'

'You see, Maurice?' exclaimed Judith. 'You see how easy you make it for them?'

'What do you mean, make it easy for them?' protested Maurice. 'I didn't even have the queen. What do you want me to do?'

'Yes, but if you did have the queen you would have covered,' persisted Judith. 'That's the point. Everyone knows it.'

Maurice sighed. 'I remember when bridge was a game that people enjoyed,' he said. 'About thirty years ago, it was. Just before we were married, in fact.'

'Let's have a break in some comfortable chairs,' suggested Miriam.

The four walked through to the lounge, taking their wine glasses with them.

'While I remember it, I heard a good joke at the office,' declared Maurice, taking his seat. 'This Samuel Isaacson is 80 years old but looks more like 90. One day he is walking – very slowly, you understand, through a dubious part of Soho.'

Miriam raised a disapproving eyebrow. Did all male jokes have to be of this nature?

'A girl standing by a doorway calls out: would you like to sleep with me for £100?'

Miriam glared at Judith. She thought it good manners to let her husband tell such jokes in polite company?

'Isaacson strokes his grey beard, uncertain whether to accept the offer,' continued Maurice. 'Making love is such an effort at my age, he tells her. But, well, I sure could do with the money!'

'Ah, sure could do with the money!' exclaimed the Cantor. 'Very good.'

'You like such jokes, Michael?' demanded Miriam.

'Er, well, not every day, but it was amusing, yes?'

Play restarted, with Miriam now occupying the South seat. This was the first hand she picked up:

♠ K   ♡ Q 10 7 5 2   ♢ K 8 6 2   ♣ 10 7 3

'One Spade,' said the Cantor, first to speak.

'Pass,' said Judith.

1NT was the bid with only 8 points, thought Miriam. Still, the spade king was not a bad card and Michael was in good form. Was it a sin to take an optimistic view once in a while? 'Two Hearts,' she said.

The Cantor's next bid was Four Clubs, a splinter bid agreeing hearts and showing at most a singleton club. 'Double,' said Judith.

A slam was not exactly what Miriam had in mind. 'Four Hearts,' she said, with almost indecent haste.

'Pass,' said Judith.

To Miriam's alarm, it seemed that Michael was considering another bid. Did he not recognise a sign-off when he heard one? Surely he would not choose this moment to overbid; he was normally such a cautious bidder.

The Cantor thumbed through his cards once more. 'Four No-trumps?' he said.

A few moments later Miriam was installed in Six Hearts, doubled by Judith. This was the full hand:

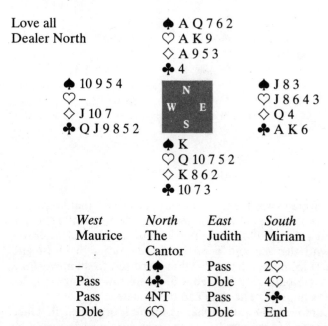

Love all
Dealer North

North
♠ A Q 7 6 2
♡ A K 9
◇ A 9 5 3
♣ 4

West
♠ 10 9 5 4
♡ –
◇ J 10 7
♣ Q J 9 8 5 2

East
♠ J 8 3
♡ J 8 6 4 3
◇ Q 4
♣ A K 6

South
♠ K
♡ Q 10 7 5 2
◇ K 8 6 2
♣ 10 7 3

West	North	East	South
Maurice	The Cantor	Judith	Miriam
–	1♠	Pass	2♡
Pass	4♣	Dble	4♡
Pass	4NT	Pass	5♣
Dble	6♡	Dble	End

Maurice led the queen of clubs and Judith overtook with the king. She continued with the ace of clubs, forcing a trump from dummy. Miriam's eyes flicked between her own hand and the cards on the table. How can Judith double this? She knew that at most one of her top clubs would stand up. She must have five trumps, surely.

At trick 3 Miriam cashed the king of spades, followed by the king and ace of diamonds. She continued with two high spades from dummy, discarding her diamond losers. These cards were still to be played:

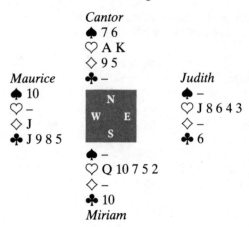

Cantor
♠ 7 6
♡ A K
♢ 9 5
♣ –

Maurice
♠ 10
♡ –
♢ J
♣ J 9 8 5

Judith
♠ –
♡ J 8 6 4 3
♢ –
♣ 6

♠ –
♡ Q 10 7 5 2
♢ –
♣ 10
Miriam

When a spade was led from dummy Judith saw that her trump pips were not strong enough for her to benefit from ruffing in. She discarded a club and Miriam ruffed with the 2. The club loser was ruffed with the ace and a further spade ruffed by East and overruffed in the South hand. Miriam crossed to dummy with a trump to the bare king and led a diamond towards her ♡ Q 10. Judith was helpless. The slam had been made.

The Cantor reached triumphantly for his scoring pencil. 'Once you responded at the two level I thought twelve tricks would be there,' he declared.

'I'm sorry, Judith,' said Maurice.

Judith eyed her husband uncertainly. 'You are sorry?' she said. 'What for?'

'I've no idea,' replied Maurice. 'The bad result must be my fault in some way, presumably.'

Judith shook her head. 'Sometimes you sound just like your father,' she said.

A few hands later Miriam was in a slam which, if successful, would give her side a large rubber.

North–South game
Dealer South

```
              ♠ K Q 5 2
              ♡ A 2
              ♢ 7 6 4
              ♣ A 7 5 2
♠ A J 10 9 3                 ♠ 8 7 4
♡ 7          N              ♡ 8 5 4
♢ 10 9 8   W   E            ♢ Q J 5 3 2
♣ Q J 8 4    S             ♣ K 9
              ♠ 6
              ♡ K Q J 10 9 6 3
              ♢ A K
              ♣ 10 6 3
```

West	North	East	South
Maurice	The Cantor	Judith	Miriam
–	–	–	1♡
1♠	3NT	Pass	4NT
Pass	5♡	Pass	6♡
All Pass			

'Four No-trumps was a limit bid?' asked Maurice, who was on lead.

'No, no, always Blackwood with Michael,' replied Miriam. 'When Judith and I play together we do something more complicated.'

The Cantor leaned forward. 'What do you mean?' he queried. 'I'm quite capable of playing the same.'

'You don't remember the last time we tried playing a complicated rule for 4NT?' said Miriam. 'That Six Diamonds against Solly Weiss?'

'Ah, yes,' replied the Cantor.

'Never again, Michael, it was too embarrassing,' said Miriam. 'Your lead, Maurice.'

Maurice led ♢10 against Six Hearts, Miriam winning with the ace. Now, how could she avoid two losers in clubs? Maurice was not the world's best defender but even he was unlikely to go in with the spade ace, setting up two winners in the dummy.

Miriam decided to postpone the play in spades, running her red suit winners first. She soon reached this position:

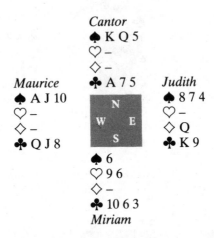

Cantor
♠ K Q 5
♡ –
♢ –
♣ A 7 5

Maurice
♠ A J 10
♡ –
♢ –
♣ Q J 8

Judith
♠ 8 7 4
♡ –
♢ Q
♣ K 9

♠ 6
♡ 9 6
♢ –
♣ 10 6 3
Miriam

On the next trump Maurice had no good card to play. If he discarded a spade declarer would throw a club from dummy; she would then lead a spade to the king and duck a spade, setting up a twelfth trick in the suit. Maurice decided to throw a club and Miriam matched this with a club from the dummy. Next came a low spade. Maurice could not afford to go in with the ace and dummy's king won the trick. Ace and another club now set a long club in the South hand. Once again Miriam had twelve tricks before her.

'Excellent play,' congratulated the Cantor. 'Pity you didn't play like that on Tuesday.'

'What was this game on Tuesday you keep mentioning?' demanded Judith.

'Don't ask, it was a disaster,' replied Miriam. 'You know Betty Zuckermann? It was a league match against her team.'

Judith looked surprised. 'They are in the first division?' she exclaimed. 'Betty can't tell one card from another.'

'Promoted last season, I don't know how,' said Miriam. 'Anyway, incredibly we lost to them. By 39 IMPs.'

'I don't believe it!' exclaimed Judith. 'Next Monday, at the synagogue ladies meeting, Betty will be unbearable.'

'I know it,' replied Miriam. 'I have had to rearrange a hair appointment, to have an excuse for not going.'

'You know what that Betty is like,' continued Judith. 'She will not let go of me until she has told me about every good board she had against you.'

Miriam glared at Judith. 'You don't have to listen to her, do you?' she said.

'Nothing could interest me less,' replied Judith. 'Still, one has to be polite in this life.'

2.   The Rabbi's Congregation

There was an excited buzz in Rothfield Hall. Tonight was no ordinary Thursday pairs. It was a heat of the nationwide Charity Simultaneous Pairs and vast numbers of masterpoints would be at stake.

'Ah, we can start against the Rabbi,' said Stan Hirsch. 'I know how you like to play against him, Gabbie. This way we can be sure.'

'Don't be silly, not in a charity,' his wife replied. 'You know how many masterpoints Myra Sakoski won in this event last year? Over 600, and she is no expert, believe me.'

Play soon began and the Rabbi had a challenging hand to play on the very first round.

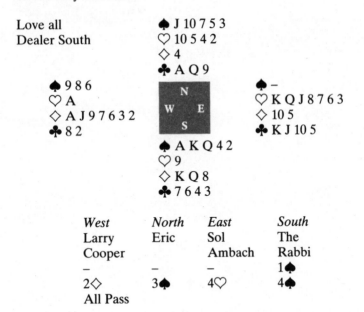

Love all
Dealer South

```
                  ♠ J 10 7 5 3
                  ♡ 10 5 4 2
                  ♢ 4
                  ♣ A Q 9
  ♠ 9 8 6                          ♠ –
  ♡ A              N               ♡ K Q J 8 7 6 3
  ♢ A J 9 7 6 3 2  W     E         ♢ 10 5
  ♣ 8 2                S           ♣ K J 10 5
                  ♠ A K Q 4 2
                  ♡ 9
                  ♢ K Q 8
                  ♣ 7 6 4 3
```

West	North	East	South
Larry	Eric	Sol	The
Cooper		Ambach	Rabbi
–	–	–	1♠
2♢	3♠	4♡	4♠
All Pass			

Larry Cooper rarely attended the synagogue and was very much what might be called a bridge-playing member. He led the ace of hearts against Four Spades and switched to ♣8. It looks as if the clubs are wrong, thought the Rabbi. Still, one club can be thrown on the diamonds. 'Play the 9, please.'

The elderly Sol Ambach won the first round of clubs with the 10 and returned ◊10 to the king and ace. When a second club was played the Rabbi rose with dummy's ace. All would now be well if trumps were 2–1; he could throw dummy's last club on the queen of diamonds, then ruff all three of his losers. The Rabbi led a trump to the ace, disappointed to see East show out. What now? A cross-ruff was no good. He could ruff two hearts high, but would be overruffed on the fourth round of the suit. Perhaps there was another way.

The Rabbi cashed the diamond queen, throwing dummy's queen of clubs. He then ruffed a diamond, East throwing a heart. A heart was ruffed high and the Rabbi then led a trump to dummy's 10. These cards remained:

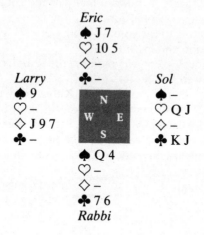

Eric
♠ J 7
♡ 10 5
◊ –
♣ –

Larry
♠ 9
♡ –
◊ J 9 7
♣ –

Sol
♠ –
♡ Q J
◊ –
♣ K J

Rabbi
♠ Q 4
♡ –
◊ –
♣ 7 6

The Rabbi had a complete count on the defenders' hands at this stage. 'Jack of trumps, please, Eric,' he said.

Sol Ambach moved his head from side to side. What to throw? If he let go a heart the Rabbi would win the trump trick with the jack, ruff a heart, then return to dummy with a club ruff. So, it must be a club.

When the Rabbi saw East's club discard he overtook the jack of trumps with the queen. He then ruffed a club in dummy, bringing down East's king. 'These are good,' he said, facing the last trump and the established club.

'What a play he makes there,' observed Larry Cooper. 'A bottom for us, you can be sure.'

'Why not support the hearts?' enquired his partner. 'With the clubs like that, we have eleven tricks.'

'Support the hearts with a singleton, he says,' exclaimed Larry Cooper. 'When I have support, I will support you.'

'Perhaps you will support us on the Shabbat, Larry,' observed the Rabbi. 'We have not seen much of you recently.'

'I come for Jahrzeit and my barmitzvah anniversary,' declared Larry Cooper. 'Also my wedding anniversary. Whenever there is an occasion, I am there.'

The Rabbi gave a sad shake of the head. 'Whenever there is an occasion,' he repeated. 'Like so many of the congregation, you have become an occasional Jew.'

The next visitors to the Rabbi's table were two great friends of his, George Kahn and his wife Hettie.

'How is business, George?' enquired the Rabbi, reaching for his cards. 'Going well?'

'Not so bad, thank you,' replied Kahn. 'But you know our Hettie, here. The more money I make, the more she spends.'

His wife nodded happily. 'It is true, I spend, spend, spend every day,' she declared. 'Typical of George to mention it, of course. Ask him to name just one other extravagance of mine and he could not do it.'

The Rabbi laughed. 'You to speak first, Hettie,' he said.

North–South game
Dealer West

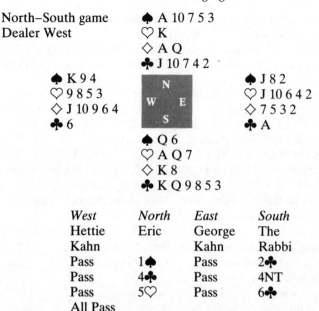

♠ A 10 7 5 3
♡ K
♢ A Q
♣ J 10 7 4 2

♠ K 9 4
♡ 9 8 5 3
♢ J 10 9 6 4
♣ 6

♠ J 8 2
♡ J 10 6 4 2
♢ 7 5 3 2
♣ A

♠ Q 6
♡ A Q 7
♢ K 8
♣ K Q 9 8 5 3

West	North	East	South
Hettie	Eric	George	The
Kahn		Kahn	Rabbi
Pass	1♠	Pass	2♣
Pass	4♣	Pass	4NT
Pass	5♡	Pass	6♣
All Pass			

Hettie Kahn led the jack of diamonds and the Rabbi surveyed the dummy with mixed feelings. There was an unfortunate duplication of values in the red suits. Against that, if trumps were 1–1 he might be able to end-play one of the defenders to open the spades.

The Rabbi won the diamond lead with dummy's ace and cashed the king of hearts. He then entered his hand by overtaking the queen of diamonds with the king. Two more rounds of hearts stood up and he exited with a trump. Both defenders followed and George Kahn won with the ace. It was clear to him that the Rabbi could not have any further cards in the red suits. He therefore tossed ♠2 on to the table.

The Rabbi paused for a moment. How to guess the spades? Suddenly he nodded to himself and played the 6 from his hand. Hettie Kahn produced the king and the Rabbi was able to claim the slam.

'What a lead you make here,' exclaimed George Kahn. 'Have you not heard of the rule: when in doubt, lead a trump?'

'I was not in doubt,' replied an affronted Hettie Kahn. 'I had a sequence in diamonds.'

George Kahn turned towards the Rabbi. 'How did you guess the spades, anyway?' he enquired. 'Put up the queen and you still go down.'

'I thought back to the bidding,' replied the Rabbi. 'With the king of spades in your hand you would perhaps have made a Lightner Double to suggest the lead of dummy's first-bid suit.'

George Kahn looked puzzled. 'Lightner Double?' he said. 'No, Hettie and I don't play it.'

The Rabbi smiled. 'If I'd known that, I might have gone down,' he replied.

'Typical of our bad luck,' declared George Kahn. 'Could you not ask, Rabbi, or look at our convention card?'

The next visitors to the Rabbi's table were Joe and Libbie Kellerman, an amiable couple in their late forties.

'I hear congratulations are in order,' declared the Rabbi. 'Your daughter is married, yes?'

Joe gave a small sigh. 'It is a mixed blessing, Rabbi,' he replied. 'As a wedding present I gave my new son-in-law a 50% share in my shoe business.'

'What a start in life!' said the Rabbi. 'Very generous of you.'

'First day after he returns from the honeymoon I put him in the sales office,' Joe continued. 'He tells me: I'm not a salesman, so I move him to the accounts department. Dad, he says. I cannot add 2 and 2 together.'

The Rabbi nodded sympathetically. 'Not so good,' he observed.

'I suggest he goes to the manufacturing division,' said Joe. 'He tells me: what do I know about making shoes? So, I confront him. I say, what do you suggest? Can you guess what he replies? Well, Dad, how about buying me out?'

The Rabbi laughed. 'He's got *chutzpah*, you must admit.'

The players drew their cards for this deal:

Love all
Dealer West

♠ 8 5 2
♡ A 7
◇ A K 9 5
♣ Q 10 9 2

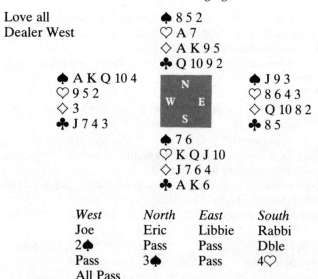

♠ A K Q 10 4
♡ 9 5 2
◇ 3
♣ J 7 4 3

♠ J 9 3
♡ 8 6 4 3
◇ Q 10 8 2
♣ 8 5

♠ 7 6
♡ K Q J 10
◇ J 7 6 4
♣ A K 6

West	North	East	South
Joe	Eric	Libbie	Rabbi
2♠	Pass	Pass	Dble
Pass	3♠	Pass	4♡
All Pass			

With no stopper in spades the Rabbi had little alternative but to bid Four Hearts on his chunky 4-card suit. Joe Kellerman led the ace of spades and down went the dummy with only two hearts. He continued with the spade king, everyone following, then the queen of spades. The Rabbi saw that if he ruffed this trick he would then need the queen of diamonds to fall in two rounds (and East to hold the fourth trump). If the diamond queen were to be so obliging, he could afford to discard on the third spade, giving himself some extra chances in the process.

The Rabbi discarded a diamond at trick 3. West then switched to a diamond. 'Ace, please,' said the Rabbi.

Trumps were drawn in four rounds and the Rabbi then played a diamond to the king, to see if the queen would fall. When West showed out on the second diamond, the Rabbi won with dummy's king. He then cashed the ace and king of clubs and continued with a finesse of ♣10. This succeeded and he was able to claim the contract.

'What bad luck we have here!' exclaimed Joe Kellerman. 'My Weak Two on a 5-card suit pushed them to a silly contract, then the Rabbi guesses the clubs correctly.'

Libbie Kellerman reached for her score-card. 'You have ever seen the Rabbi misguess a suit?'

The Rabbi smiled. 'What is this word: guess?' he said. 'When Joe has shown me five spades, three hearts and one diamond, it is a guess to play him for four clubs?'

'Ah, you take all the magic from the play,' replied Libbie Kellerman. 'It is like seeing a clever conjuring trick. Once you know how it is done, you lose interest.'

'Most good bridge is just a matter of hard work,' declared the Rabbi. 'In that respect, it is like life.'

Joe Kellerman nodded. 'Tell that to my son-in-law,' he observed.

The Rabbi and Eric picked up a mixture of good and bad results on the next few rounds, then Sam and David arrived.

'You are not playing with your wife, David?' enquired the Rabbi.

David took his seat. 'I never knew what true happiness was until I got married,' he said. 'And by then it was too late.'

'What is the problem?' enquired the Rabbi.

'Only the usual,' replied David. 'All day, every day, she is trying to correct my faults.'

Sam spread his hands. 'It shows how much she loves you, David,' he said.

'Sam is right,' declared the Rabbi. 'The happiest Jewish wife is not the one who marries the best man, it is the one who makes the best man out of the man she married.'

The Rabbi cast an eye over these cards:

♠ A 10 8 6 3   ♡ A 7   ◇ 10 7 4 3   ♣ Q 8

'One Heart,' said David, to his left.

'Two no-trumps,' said Eric. This was the Unusual No-trump, showing length in both the minor suits.

'Three Hearts,' said Sam.

The Rabbi inspected the vulnerability. Game All. So, Eric should have good suits. Could anyone with red blood in his veins bid only Four Diamonds with both major aces and such trump support? 'Five Diamonds,' said the Rabbi.

There was no further bidding. David led the king of hearts and down went the dummy.

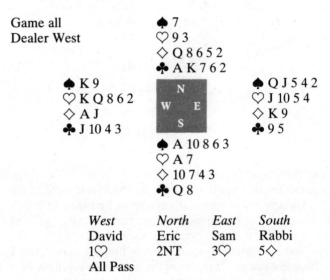

Game all
Dealer West

♠ 7
♡ 9 3
◇ Q 8 6 5 2
♣ A K 7 6 2

♠ K 9
♡ K Q 8 6 2
◇ A J
♣ J 10 4 3

♠ Q J 5 4 2
♡ J 10 5 4
◇ K 9
♣ 9 5

♠ A 10 8 6 3
♡ A 7
◇ 10 7 4 3
♣ Q 8

West	North	East	South
David	Eric	Sam	Rabbi
1♡	2NT	3♡	5◇
All Pass			

'I did not see we were vulnerable,' observed Eric. 'Still, the clubs are good.'

If the diamonds were as good as the clubs I would be in business, thought the Rabbi. What to do? Apart from the horrible trumps, there was now a top heart loser.

The Rabbi won the heart lead with the ace and turned to the club suit, hoping to discard his losing heart. The defenders followed to the first two clubs but East ruffed the third round with the 9. The Rabbi overruffed with the 10, cashed the ace of spades, and re-entered dummy with a spade ruff. He then led a fourth round of clubs.

It would not assist East to ruff with the bare king, since declarer would throw his heart loser. Sam threw a heart himself and the Rabbi ruffed in the South hand. He now led a third round of spades. West saw he could not gain by ruffing, and the spade was ruffed in the dummy. These cards remained:

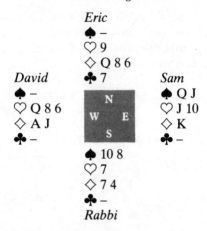

Eric
♠ –
♡ 9
♢ Q 8 6
♣ 7

David
♠ –
♡ Q 8 6
♢ A J
♣ –

Sam
♠ Q J
♡ J 10
♢ K
♣ –

Rabbi
♠ 10 8
♡ 7
♢ 7 4
♣ –

'Play the club,' said the Rabbi.

East discarded a heart and so did the Rabbi. David ruffed with the jack of trumps and returned the queen of hearts. The Rabbi ruffed in the South hand, then led a trump. The defenders' ace and king fell to the baize and the game had been made.

Sam nodded his appreciation of the fine dummy play. 'And I guess the happiest bridge player is not the one who is given the best dummy,' he observed. 'It is the one who makes the best out of the dummy received.'

On the penultimate round of the event Miriam and the Cantor arrived at the Rabbi's table.

'That visitor playing with Lionel Berg, he just told me a passable joke,' said the Cantor, taking his seat. 'About the town overrun with mice. You have heard it?'

'Not that I recall,' replied the Rabbi.

'The inhabitants advertised for someone to rid the town of mice,' said the Cantor, 'and their call was answered by a Rabbi.'

'Amazing.'

'Even more amazing,' continued the Cantor, 'is that the Rabbi was completely successful in his task.'

'And how did he manage it?'

'Apparently he gave all the mice a Barmitzvah,' replied the Cantor. 'Naturally, after that they were never seen again.'

'Very good,' replied the Rabbi with a smile. 'And in these times all too appropriate.'

The players drew their cards for this deal:

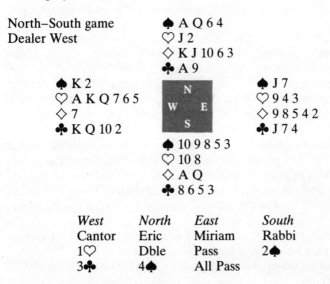

North–South game
Dealer West

♠ A Q 6 4
♡ J 2
♢ K J 10 6 3
♣ A 9

♠ K 2
♡ A K Q 7 6 5
♢ 7
♣ K Q 10 2

♠ J 7
♡ 9 4 3
♢ 9 8 5 4 2
♣ J 7 4

♠ 10 9 8 5 3
♡ 10 8
♢ A Q
♣ 8 6 5 3

West	North	East	South
Cantor	Eric	Miriam	Rabbi
1♡	Dble	Pass	2♠
3♣	4♠	All Pass	

The Rabbi was barely worth his jump to Two Spades and a borderline spade game was reached. The Cantor cashed the ace and king of hearts, then switched to the king of clubs. The Rabbi won with dummy's ace of clubs and crossed to his hand with a diamond to the ace. When he played a trump to the queen Miriam defended cleverly by contributing a smooth jack.

The key moment of the hand had arrived. If the Rabbi read the jack as a singleton, he would attempt to reach his hand in diamonds to run ♠10 through West's presumed ♠K 7. The Cantor would in fact ruff the second diamond and cash a club. That would be one down.

'Ace of trumps, please,' said the Rabbi.

Miriam tossed her remaining trump onto the table and the king fell from West. The Rabbi was able to discard three clubs on dummy's diamond suit and ended with an overtrick.

'Such a clever defence I made there,' declared Miriam. 'Did you not see you could pick up Michael's ♠Kx by crossing in diamonds?'

'I saw it, of course,' replied the Rabbi, 'but I saw also that a diamond ruff was certain in that case. Michael has bid hearts and clubs; if he does have three trumps, there is room for only one diamond.'

Miriam glared across the table. 'So, these clubs had to be bid, Michael?' she said. 'You could not think perhaps to rebid Three Hearts, to allow my brilliant defence to work?'

The Cantor, who would do or say anything for a peaceful life, returned his cards to the wallet. 'Yes, perhaps Three Hearts would have been better,' he replied.

Stan and Gabbie Hirsch had been enjoying a fine session. 'For the last round we are at Table 8, East–West,' said Gabbie excitedly. 'Let us pray it is not the Rabbi. With a score-card like this, the masterpoints will descend like confetti at a wedding.'

'Ah, Stan and Gabbie, my friends,' exclaimed the Rabbi, as the last pair arrived at his table. 'I thought we weren't going to see you.'

Gabbie maintained an impassive expression as she took her seat. 'That would have been a pity,' she said.

'Your grandson has started school, yes?' continued the Rabbi.

'Only five years old and such business sense he has already,' replied Stan Hirsch, chuckling to himself.

'How do you mean?' queried the Rabbi.

'On his first day the teacher asked him to name the four seasons,' replied Hirsch. 'He tells her she is wrong. There are only two – busy and slack!'

'That boy will go far,' declared the Rabbi.

The Rabbi and Eric defended tidily on the first board of the round, holding Stan Hirsch to only +90 in 1NT. Gabbie was looking for better things on the final board. With the score at Game All she picked up these cards:

♠ Q 2　　♡ Q 6 4　　♢ K 10 3 2　　♣ Q 10 5 3

'One Spade,' said Stan Hirsch, first to speak.

Eric passed and Gabbie Hirsch surveyed her 9-count. Too much of a stretch to respond at the two-level, she thought. In any case, Stan always played the cards poorly against the Rabbi. Best to be first to bid no-trumps. 'One no-trump,' she said.

The Rabbi entered with Three Diamonds, Stan rebid Four Spades, and Eric bid Five Diamonds.

Visions of a heavily-inscribed masterpoint certificate re-appeared before Gabbie's eyes. 'Double!' she said.

There was no further bidding and her husband led the ace of spades. This was the full deal:

Game all
Dealer West

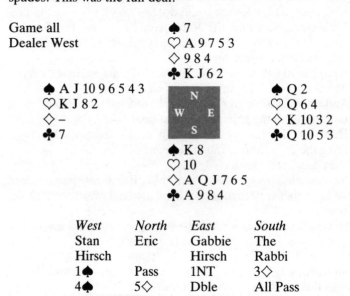

```
                        ♠ 7
                        ♡ A 9 7 5 3
                        ◇ 9 8 4
                        ♣ K J 6 2
    ♠ A J 10 9 6 5 4 3                    ♠ Q 2
    ♡ K J 8 2                             ♡ Q 6 4
    ◇ -                                   ◇ K 10 3 2
    ♣ 7                                   ♣ Q 10 5 3
                        ♠ K 8
                        ♡ 10
                        ◇ A Q J 7 6 5
                        ♣ A 9 8 4
```

West	North	East	South
Stan	Eric	Gabbie	The
Hirsch		Hirsch	Rabbi
1♠	Pass	1NT	3◇
4♠	5◇	Dble	All Pass

The ace of spades won the first trick and West switched to a low heart, won with dummy's ace. How can the opponents bid so much with so few points between them, wondered the Rabbi. Surely the trumps must be 4–0. Gabbie would not double him with only king-to-three trumps sitting under the main holding. 'Nine of diamonds, please,' said the Rabbi.

East played low and the 9 was run successfully, West discarding a spade. Next came the 8 of diamonds, covered by the 10 and queen. The Rabbi now turned his eye to the club suit. All would be well if the clubs divided 3–2. West was marked with eight spades, however. Suppose his shape was 8–4–0–1 and his club singleton was a low one. Declarer would then need two entries to dummy, one to pick up East's king of trumps, the other to finesse against her second club honour.

After a few moments calculation the Rabbi led ♣9 from his hand, running it to East's 10. He then ruffed the heart return and led ♣8 to dummy's king, West showing out. The Rabbi gave a learned nod of the head. 'Play the jack of clubs,' he said.

After the Rabbi's masterly handling of the club pips, there was nothing that Gabbie Hirsch could do. She chose to cover the jack with the queen but now the Rabbi could overtake his ♣4 with dummy's 6. A trump to the jack picked up East's king and declarer had eleven tricks before him.

'What a lead you make here!' exclaimed Gabbie Hirsch. 'Without the ace of spades lead he has no chance.'

'And what a double you make here!' retorted Stan Hirsch. 'You think he will run the trump 9 without your double?'

'They should not even be in Five Diamonds,' continued his wife, entering the disastrous −750 in her card. 'Open Four Spades and they are shut out. Quite cold, it is.'

'Not completely,' observed the Rabbi. 'Eric would perhaps lead ace of hearts and another heart; then I can underlead the club ace for a second ruff.'

'Of course, for them it would be very clever to lead a major-suit ace,' said Stan Hirsch. 'For me it is stupid.'

The Rabbi smiled at his two old friends. 'No need to worry about it, anyway,' he said. 'It's only a meaningless Charity event. Who in this room cares how well they do?'

3.   Miriam's Easy Draw

'One thing has always puzzled me,' declared Miriam, checking her lipstick in the mirror. 'Why are women so much better than men at bridge?'

'Men aren't mentally inferior, if you believe the scientists,' replied Judith. 'It must be because they have other things on their mind. You know, their work, their cars, all those stupid sports.'

Miriam nodded. 'You can't believe what Michael did to me the other night,' she said. 'I made a vulnerable overcall of Two Hearts and the opponents bid to 3NT. Can you guess what he led?'

Judith thought for a few moments. 'The jack of clubs?' she suggested.

Miriam's mouth dropped. 'How did you know?' she said.

'You phoned to tell me immediately after the game,' replied Judith. 'Half past eleven it was! A few years ago, you might have interrupted something at such a time.'

Miriam gave a small sigh. 'I have the same problem with Michael,' she said.

Becky and Rachel soon arrived and the four set off in Miriam's car for a Crockford's Cup match. The team was in the middle of a very successful season. Miriam and Judith drew the best from themselves by trying to out-play each other. Becky and Rachel were equally successful in a different way. Great personal friends, they supported each other through good moments and bad – always sympathetic when any mistakes were made.

'Who is this team we're playing?' enquired Judith. 'Do you know if they're any good?'

'I don't imagine so,' replied Miriam, sounding the horn as a car pulled out in front of her. 'They have no women in the team, anyway.'

The four arrived in good time at Bill Hutson's large detached house in Surrey's stockbroker belt. The match was a few boards old when Miriam picked up these cards:

♠ 4   ♡ Q J 10 9 7   ♢ A 8 4 2   ♣ K 7 5

'One Club,' said the white-haired Doctor Moore.

'One Spade,' said Judith.

'Pass,' said John Baines, a short man with pebble-lensed glasses.

What to do, thought Miriam. If Judith had her usual ♠K Q J x x and a side jack, they were high enough already. Still, was it impossible that they had a heart fit? Surely it could not hurt to go just one level higher. 'Two Hearts,' said Miriam.

Judith raised to Three Hearts and, realising she had little justification for the call, Miriam made it Four Hearts. West led the king of diamonds and the cards lay like this:

North–South game
Dealer West

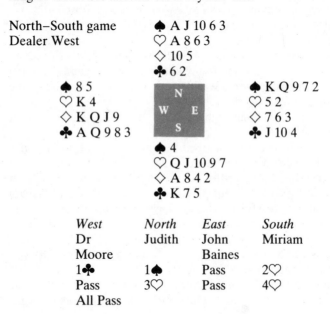

        ♠ A J 10 6 3
        ♡ A 8 6 3
        ◇ 10 5
        ♣ 6 2

♠ 8 5　　　　　　　　　　♠ K Q 9 7 2
♡ K 4　　　　　　　　　　♡ 5 2
◇ K Q J 9　　　　　　　　◇ 7 6 3
♣ A Q 9 8 3　　　　　　　♣ J 10 4

        ♠ 4
        ♡ Q J 10 9 7
        ◇ A 8 4 2
        ♣ K 7 5

West	*North*	*East*	*South*
Dr	Judith	John	Miriam
Moore		Baines	
1♣	1♠	Pass	2♡
Pass	3♡	Pass	4♡
All Pass			

Miriam won the diamond lead with the ace. The ace of clubs was surely offside, so it seemed that the only real hope was to establish dummy's spades. She crossed to the ace of spades at trick 2 and ruffed a spade. The queen of trumps was run successfully and a second round cleared the defenders' trumps.

When Miriam ruffed a second spade in her hand the news was less good, West showing out. So much for setting up the spades, she thought. It looks like down one. Better give up a diamond, to prepare for two diamond ruffs.

Miriam led a diamond towards the dummy's bare 10 and West went in with the jack. He was on lead in this end position:

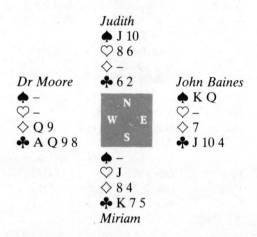

Judith
♠ J 10
♡ 8 6
♢ –
♣ 6 2

Dr Moore
♠ –
♡ –
♢ Q 9
♣ A Q 9 8

John Baines
♠ K Q
♡ –
♢ 7
♣ J 10 4

Miriam
♠ –
♡ J
♢ 8 4
♣ K 7 5

Doctor Moore led the queen of diamonds and Miriam was on the point of ruffing this card when inspiration struck. Of course! If she discarded clubs from dummy on West's master diamonds, he would then be end-played. 'Club away,' said Miriam.

West produced another high diamond and Miriam threw dummy's last club. When Doctor Moore exited with a low club. Miriam ran it to her king. She could then claim the balance.

'What a strange hand,' exclaimed the Doctor. 'I made three diamond tricks but nothing else.'

Miriam caught Judith's eye. After a sparkling play like that, would a small compliment be out of order?

Judith reached for her score-card. 'Just the ten, was it?' she said.

Meanwhile, in the Hutsons' capacious drawing room, the opponents had just reached a grand slam.

Love all   ♠ A Q 10 7
Dealer North   ♡ K J 5 2
                        ◇ A K 10 4
                        ♣ 6

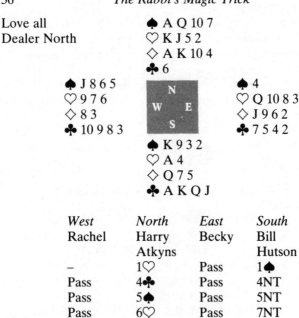

♠ J 8 6 5   ♠ 4
♡ 9 7 6   ♡ Q 10 8 3
◇ 8 3   ◇ J 9 6 2
♣ 10 9 8 3   ♣ 7 5 4 2

                        ♠ K 9 3 2
                        ♡ A 4
                        ◇ Q 7 5
                        ♣ A K Q J

West	North	East	South
Rachel	Harry	Becky	Bill
	Atkyns		Hutson
–	1♡	Pass	1♠
Pass	4♣	Pass	4NT
Pass	5♠	Pass	5NT
Pass	6♡	Pass	7NT
All Pass			

North showed his spade support with a splinter bid in clubs. Keycard Blackwood then revealed that he held two aces, the queen of spades, and two outside kings. The florid-complexioned Bill Hutson arrived in 7NT and Rachel led ♣10.

'Very nice, Harry,' said Bill Hutson, as he inspected the dummy. 'We bid it well.'

Hutson won the club lead with the ace and played a spade to the ace, Rachel contributing the 8 from the West seat. 'That was the 8, was it?' he said, before quitting the trick.

Rachel faced the card impassively. Bill Hutson smiled to himself. If a man had produced the 8 he would have suspected a false card from jack–8 to four. It was so much easier playing against female opposition. 'Queen of spades, please,' he said.

The appearance of a small club from East was not exactly what Hutson had been hoping for. He reached his hand with the queen of diamonds and cashed three more rounds of clubs, throwing two spades and a heart from dummy. Becky, in the East seat, discarded a heart, matching dummy's length in the red suits. Three rounds of diamonds failed to drop the jack and when declarer eventually fell back on the heart finesse, that failed too. The grand was one down.

'Luck of the Devil, we had there!' declared Bill Hutson. 'Must have been around a 95% contract.'

His partner gave an annoyed shake of the head. 'I expect they'll stop in six in the other room,' he said.

The prediction proved wide of the mark. 'Plus 1520,' said Miriam, as scores were compared for the first time.

'You made 7NT?' exclaimed Rachel. 'How did the play go?'

'No problem, was there?' replied Miriam. 'I tested the diamonds and cashed the top cards in clubs and hearts. East had four clubs, four diamonds and at least two hearts . . . so, he couldn't hold four spades.'

'Brilliant!' exclaimed Becky. 'So you knew how to play the spades.'

Judith scribbled 19 IMPs into the plus column. 'Nothing brilliant about it,' she said. 'Only a man could go down.'

The home team played a sound game in the next two sets and the ladies led by just 7 IMPs at the half-time refreshment break.

'Did you make this quiche yourself?' enquired Miriam, failing to bite through the rock-hard pastry.

'No, no, it's from the supermarket,' replied Bill Hutson. 'Reduced to half price for some reason.'

Having witnessed this exchange, Judith declined a piece of quiche. She took a sip of her coffee instead, wincing at the taste. They still made instant coffee? Surely everyone ground their own beans nowadays?

The disappointing fare did not delay matters for long and the third set started with Judith and Miriam facing the doctor and his partner. Miriam was soon put to the test.

North–South game
Dealer South

♠ Q 9 3
♡ A Q 10
◇ J 8 5
♣ 6 4 3 2

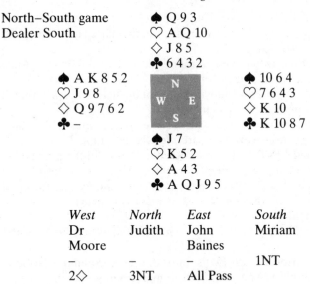

♠ A K 8 5 2
♡ J 9 8
◇ Q 9 7 6 2
♣ —

♠ 10 6 4
♡ 7 6 4 3
◇ K 10
♣ K 10 8 7

♠ J 7
♡ K 5 2
◇ A 4 3
♣ A Q J 9 5

West	North	East	South
Dr	Judith	John	Miriam
Moore		Baines	
–	–	–	1NT
2◇	3NT	All Pass	

Miriam opened a 15–17 1NT and Doctor Moore entered with an Aspro overcall, showing spades and a minor. Judith was worth only a raise to 2NT but, when partnering Miriam, it was her custom to respond 3NT on borderline hands. If the contract failed, she would be there with a superior 'One down, partner?'. If the contract succeeded, well, there would at least be the consolation of a good board.

West led ♣5 against 3NT and Miriam won in hand with the jack. What to do? It seemed she would have to bring in the club suit.

Miriam crossed to the queen of hearts and played a club to the queen. Good news and bad news. The finesse succeeded but West showed out, revealing the 4–0 break. The club suit could still be picked up, but only if Miriam could cross twice more to dummy. She gritted her teeth. It seemed she would have to risk a finesse of dummy's ♡10. There was no other way.

Miriam led a low heart from her hand. After a few seconds pause, Doctor Moore contributed a purposeful jack to the trick. This forced the ace, leaving dummy's 10 facing declarer's bare king. With the extra entry in the suit killed, it was no longer possible to pick up the club suit. The contract went down.

'Oh yes, brilliant defence!' congratulated John Baines, peering through his thick lenses. 'They write about these blocking plays in books but I don't think I've ever seen one at the table before.'

'If declarer foresees the position, she can overtake the king of hearts with the ace on the first round,' observed Doctor Moore.

Judith blinked. Had Miriam misplayed the hand?

'That would be clever,' Baines replied. 'If clubs are 2–2 or 3–1 you only need two heart tricks. If they're 4–0, you clear the way for a finesse of the heart 10.'

Judith glared across the table. 'Overtake the king of hearts with the ace,' she said. 'Then you can finesse the 10.'

'Do I have a parrot for a partner?' retorted Miriam. 'Do you think I cannot hear what they say the first time?'

'No need to be rude just because you misplay a hand,' muttered Judith.

At the other table Rachel was about to lead against a small slam. Somewhat unusually, she held two aces in her hand. This was the deal:

Game all
Dealer West

```
                    ♠ A K 8 4
                    ♡ K Q J 4 2
                    ◇ Q J 9 7
                    ♣ —
   ♠ J 7                              ♠ 10 9 5 2
   ♡ 7              N                 ♡ 9 8 6 5 3
   ◇ A 10 5 2    W     E              ◇ —
   ♣ A 9 7 4 3 2     S               ♣ J 10 8 6
                    ♠ Q 6 3
                    ♡ A 10
                    ◇ K 8 6 4 3
                    ♣ K Q 5
```

West	North	East	South
Rachel	Harry	Becky	Bill
	Atkyns		Hutson
Pass	1♡	Pass	2◇
Pass	4♣	Pass	4♡
Pass	4♠	Pass	5◇
Pass	6◇	All Pass	

'The Four Club bid?' enquired Rachel.

Bill Hutson, an impatient man whose face had become progressively redder as the match progressed, stared back at her. 'It was a splinter bid,' he replied. 'You don't play them?'

'I thought it might be Gerber,' said Rachel.

Bill Hutson let out a loud laugh. 'This isn't the local church hall,' he retorted. 'I don't think you'll find anyone using Gerber at this stage of Crockford's.'

'We play it,' said Becky.

Rachel looked at her hand once more, still undecided what to lead. Why had North advanced to a slam despite his partner's sign-off? Since he was missing both the minor-suit aces, it could only be because his splinter bid was based on a void club rather than a singleton club. Yes, and in that case it might be possible to weaken the dummy's trump holding with a rather unusual lead.

Her heart pounding, Rachel led ♣4.

Bill Hutson nodded approvingly as he surveyed the dummy. 'Ruff low,' he said. 'And the queen of trumps, please.'

East showed out on the first round of trumps. Rachel won with the ace and, after a moment's pause to savour the moment, continued with the ace of clubs. Bill Hutson stared at the card in disbelief. There was nothing he could do. He had to ruff for a second time in the dummy and it was no longer possible to pick up West's 10 of trumps. The slam was one down.

'Brilliant lead, Rachel,' congratulated Becky. 'How did you work it out?'

Rachel smiled back happily. 'Fourth best of the longest and strongest,' she replied.

Bill Hutson eyed Rachel uncertainly. If a man had made such a lead he would have been the first to congratulate him. A woman, though? It was hardly conceivable that she had known what she was doing. 'Nothing wrong with our bidding, Harry,' he said. 'Any other lead and I make it easily.'

With eight boards left to play, the ladies were in the lead by 11 IMPs. This was the critical board of the last set:

East–West game   ♠ A J 9 7 4
Dealer South   ♡ 9 5
                    ◇ Q 9
                    ♣ 10 6 4 2

♠ 10 8 5 3		♠ –
♡ K 10 8 3 2	**N**	♡ Q J 7 4
◇ J 10 8	**W E**	◇ 7 5 4 3 2
♣ Q	**S**	♣ J 9 8 3

                  ♠ K Q 6 2
                  ♡ A 6
                  ◇ A K 6
                  ♣ A K 7 5

West	*North*	*East*	*South*
Harry	Judith	Bill	Miriam
Atkyns		Hutson	
–	–	–	2♣
Pass	2◇	Pass	2NT
Pass	3♡	Pass	4♠
Pass	4NT	Pass	5◇
Pass	6♠	All Pass	

With her splendid fit for spades, Miriam jumped to Four Spades over her partner's transfer response. Roman Key-Card Black-wood identified that South held three aces and the trump king and Judith bid the slam.

Since it was likely that the opponents held all four aces, Harry Atkyns decided not to lead his singleton club. He led ◇J and Miriam won with dummy's queen. The slam was a good one, despite the modest point-count. Even if the clubs broke 4–1, there would be various chances. 'Ace of trumps, please,' she said.

When East showed out, discarding a diamond, prospects were not quite so good. Miriam drew all the trumps, East throwing four diamonds, then cashed the diamond ace–king, East throwing two hearts. These cards remained:

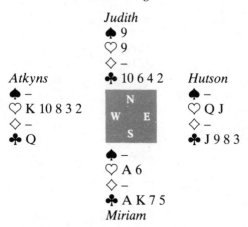

Judith
♠ 9
♡ 9
♢ –
♣ 10 6 4 2

Atkyns
♠ –
♡ K 10 8 3 2
♢ –
♣ Q

Hutson
♠ –
♡ Q J
♢ –
♣ J 9 8 3

Miriam
♠ –
♡ A 6
♢ –
♣ A K 7 5

When the ace of clubs was played, the queen fell on the left. Not the best of omens, thought Miriam. The queen on the right, that would have been different. How did the club lie? If West had started with ♣Q J doubleton she could score an overtrick by simply laying down the club king. What if the queen was a singleton? In that case East would now be down to two hearts and ♣J 9 8. Miriam's eyes lit up. In that case it would be possible to end-play him! Ace of hearts, ruff a heart, then duck a club.

Miriam stole a glance at the red-faced Bill Hutson. He was looking quietly contented with life, not at all like a man who was expecting to lose a bundle of IMPs when the opponents succeeded in a thin slam. Surely he knew that the clubs were breaking badly and thought the slam could not be made.

Miriam cashed the ace of hearts and ruffed a heart, bringing down the queen and the jack from East. Certain that she had made the right decision, she played a club from dummy, ducking when East's 8 appeared. West showed out and Miriam faced her remaining cards exultantly. 'Twelve tricks,' she said.

'That's one mistake too many, Bill,' observed Harry Atkyns, thrusting his cards back into the wallet. 'You should come down to four clubs and a diamond. Then you can throw a club when declarer ruffs the heart at the end. You make the setting trick in diamonds.'

'You think I should throw the queen–jack of hearts to keep five diamonds to the 7?' demanded Bill Hutson, his complexion edging to a dangerous shade of red. 'Is that what you're suggesting?'

'I didn't say it was easy,' Atkyns replied. 'I don't see how else we can beat it, though.'

The ladies had won the match by a comfortable 29 IMPs and Miriam's green Rover was soon threading its way through the late-night traffic.

'We're in the last sixteen now, aren't we?' exclaimed Becky, leaning forward excitedly from one of the back seats. 'I wonder who we'll play in the next round.'

'We can't expect another easy draw like that,' declared Miriam, accelerating to beat the changing traffic lights. 'When you reach the last sixteen of a national event the teams are certain to have women in them.'

4.   David's Miracle

'Well, it worked again,' said David, arriving at the Rabbi's house for a men's four.

'What's that?' enquired the Rabbi.

'I had to take a taxi here tonight,' replied David. 'As I am getting out I fumble in my pockets, then start searching the floor. Finally I say to the driver: I have dropped a 50-pound note on the floor. Wait here, please, while I borrow a torch to look for it.'

'So?' said the Rabbi.

'The moment I take two steps away from the cab, off it goes at full speed! Another free trip.'

'A sad indictment of human nature,' declared the Rabbi. 'For cab drivers and for you.'

Sam and Eric arrived on time and the game began. The Rabbi was a notoriously lucky card-holder and it was no surprise to him when he immediately picked up this fine collection:

♠ A 4   ♥ A K 10 9 8 3   ♦ K 6 2   ♣ Q 4

'One No-trump,' said David, first to speak.

Even better, thought the Rabbi. My partner opens. With 12–14 points opposite, there must be chances of a slam. 'Three Hearts,' he said.

David consulted his hand learnedly. 'Four Clubs,' he said.

So, a maximum with heart support. The Rabbi inspected his hand once more. Could there be a grand on? The diamond ace and ♣A K J x would be enough. Still, best to be conservative in this world. 'Six Hearts,' said the Rabbi.

Eric led ♣10 and this was the full deal:

Love all
Dealer North

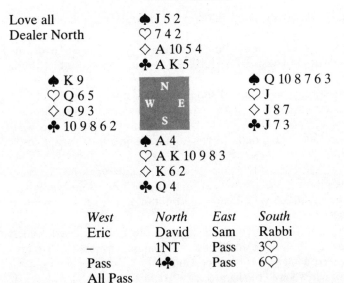

♠ J 5 2
♡ 7 4 2
◇ A 10 5 4
♣ A K 5

♠ K 9
♡ Q 6 5
◇ Q 9 3
♣ 10 9 8 6 2

♠ Q 10 8 7 6 3
♡ J
◇ J 8 7
♣ J 7 3

♠ A 4
♡ A K 10 9 8 3
◇ K 6 2
♣ Q 4

West	North	East	South
Eric	*David*	*Sam*	*Rabbi*
–	1NT	Pass	3♡
Pass	4♣	Pass	6♡
All Pass			

'You see how I remember the system you like?' exclaimed
David proudly. 'Four Clubs to show the ace and a good fit for
hearts.'

Better perhaps to forget the system, thought the Rabbi, on a
9-loser hand with only three small trumps. Still, with his own hand
so strong the slam was a good one.

The Rabbi won the club lead with the queen and cashed the ace
of trumps, the jack falling from East. That jack looks like a
singleton, he thought. What to do in that case? Perhaps there was
a chance if the diamonds divided 3–3. The Rabbi crossed to the
ace of diamonds and played a diamond towards the king. Both
defenders followed and he continued with two more rounds of
clubs, discarding a diamond. He then ruffed a diamond with the
10, finding the suit 3–3.

The Rabbi gave a satisfied nod. Instead of cashing the king of
trumps next, he led the 8 of trumps from hand. If Eric were
to duck, he would wave goodbye to his trump trick. Eventually
he decided to win with the queen and exit with a third round
of trumps. In dummy with the trump 7 the Rabbi discarded his

spade loser on the long diamond. He could then claim twelve tricks.

'What a lead you make here!' exclaimed Sam. 'Lead a spade and we beat it. If I wanted a club lead I would have doubled Four Clubs.'

Eric spread his hands. 'I should lead from king doubleton?' he protested. 'Against a game, maybe. Not against a slam.'

Sam turned towards the Rabbi. 'Why do you play it this way, anyway?' he demanded. 'Might I not have queen–jack doubleton of trumps?'

'Yes, but if you do I cannot be overruffed in diamonds,' replied the Rabbi. 'Even if you ruff the third club winner it is not necessarily disastrous. I can overruff and play for three diamond tricks.'

Eric, not overjoyed at having his opening lead criticised, joined in the fray. 'Single jack is twice as likely as queen–jack doubleton,' he declared. 'It was Restricted Choice.'

'Not when I hold the hand,' retorted Sam. 'You think a player of my experience would not false-card the jack from queen–jack doubleton? Automatic, it is. Absolutely automatic.'

'Changing the subject,' said the Rabbi, 'did you hear the Goldenbergers' news?'

'She is expecting around now, yes?'

'Not any more,' replied the Rabbi. 'She has had triplets! Can you believe it?'

'Unusual, indeed,' said David. 'They say it happens only once every 200,000 times.'

Sam raised an eyebrow at this. 'No wonder he never has any time for his business,' he declared.

A few nondescript hands brought the score to Game All. The Rabbi then picked up this hand:

♠ A Q 4   ♡ A K Q 5   ◇ A 8 7   ♣ A 6 4

After a start of 2♣–2◇–2NT, David introduced a Stayman 3♣.

'Three Hearts,' said the Rabbi.

'Five Hearts,' said David.

Well, the shape was not good, thought the Rabbi, but how often did partner make a slam try when you held four aces and the king–queen of trumps? In fact, it was lucky David had not bid Roman Key-card Blackwood! For the moment he could not remember what the answer would be, with all the key cards.

The Rabbi raised to Six Hearts and this was the full layout:

Game all
Dealer South

	♠ 10 5 2	
	♡ 7 6 3 2	
	◇ K Q 6 5 4	
	♣ 5	

West		East
♠ K 8	N	♠ J 9 7 6 3
♡ J 10 8 4	W E	♡ 9
◇ 9 2	S	◇ J 10 3
♣ Q J 10 8 2		♣ K 9 7 3

	♠ A Q 4	
	♡ A K Q 5	
	◇ A 8 7	
	♣ A 6 4	

West	North	East	South
Eric	David	Sam	Rabbi
–	–	–	2♣
Pass	2◇	Pass	2NT
Pass	3♣	Pass	3♡
Pass	5♡	Pass	6♡
All Pass			

Eric led the queen of clubs against Six Hearts and the Rabbi won with the ace. If both red suits broke favourably, he thought, thirteen tricks would be easy. What if the trumps were 4–1? If he cashed two rounds of trumps and someone showed out, he could take two club ruffs but then the defender with the long trump would be able to stop the flow of the diamonds. Yes, best to give up a trump trick early, as a safeguard.

The Rabbi led ♡5 from the South hand and Sam, sitting East, won with the 9. He switched to a spade and the Rabbi rose with his ace. Now came ace of clubs, club ruff, ace of trumps (East showing out), and a second club ruff. The Rabbi returned to his hand with the trump king and drew West's last trump. When the diamond suit divided 3–2 he had twelve tricks.

'So, you would have liked me to lead from king doubleton spade on that hand?' asked Eric. 'The lead would make it easy for him.'

Sam shrugged his shoulders. 'Easy, difficult, it makes no difference,' he replied. 'Not when the Rabbi is playing the hand.'

For the next rubber Sam cut to partner David, a player of whom he had a very low opinion. David's mind seemed to be elsewhere as he shuffled laboriously for the first deal. 'I read an interesting article in the *Telegraph* this morning, Rabbi,' he said. 'It asked the reader what he would choose to do if he had only 15 minutes left to live'.

'Only 15 minutes?' said the Rabbi. 'I think I'd shuffle a little faster.'

On the first deal Sam picked up these cards:

♠ A Q J 6 4 3   ♡ 7 6   ◇ K Q 4   ♣ 5 3

'No bid,' said the Rabbi, first to speak.

'One no-trump,' said David. This was a weak no-trump, showing 12–14 points.

Eric passed and Sam had to consider his response. Of course, to protect those two doubletons from the opening lead it was right to make a transfer response. But any trick saved in that respect would doubtless be thrown away by David in the later play. It was certainly tempting to respond Four Spades and play the contract himself.

'Your bid, Sam,' said the Rabbi.

Ah well, thought Sam, it is not as though the stakes are high. 'Two Hearts,' he said.

David bid a dutiful Two Spades and Sam raised to Four Spades. Eric led the ace of hearts and this was the complete deal:

Love all
Dealer East

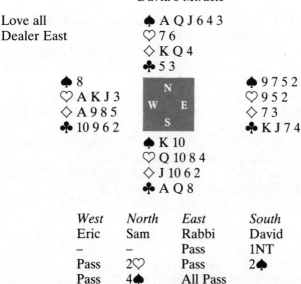

♠ A Q J 6 4 3
♡ 7 6
◇ K Q 4
♣ 5 3

♠ 8
♡ A K J 3
◇ A 9 8 5
♣ 10 9 6 2

♠ 9 7 5 2
♡ 9 5 2
◇ 7 3
♣ K J 7 4

♠ K 10
♡ Q 10 8 4
◇ J 10 6 2
♣ A Q 8

West	North	East	South
Eric	*Sam*	*Rabbi*	*David*
–	–	Pass	1NT
Pass	2♡	Pass	2♠
Pass	4♠	All Pass	

'Two Hearts seems obvious on your hand,' observed the Rabbi. 'You were thinking of bidding 3NT instead?'

'Er . . . yes, 3NT could be right,' replied Sam.

On the first round of hearts Rabbi contributed the 9, hoping to look like a man with a doubleton in the suit. Eric duly continued with king of hearts, the Rabbi completing his peter, and another heart.

David was looking worried. He still had to lose a diamond trick, so he could not afford to suffer an overruff. With a purposeful air he reached for dummy's jack of trumps.

When the Rabbi produced another heart Sam looked scornfully towards his partner. 'You were born yesterday, David?' he said.

David played a trump to the king and continued with the 10 of trumps. When West showed out, declarer could not afford to overtake in trumps. The 10 won the trick and he next played a low diamond.

Eric was alert to the situation. He rose with the ace of diamonds and played a fourth round of hearts. The Rabbi's 9 of trumps was promoted and the game was one down.

'With A K Q J 10 of trumps you lose a trump trick?' exclaimed Sam. 'Is that good play, do you think?'

'I did everything possible to avoid the loss of a trump trick,' replied David. 'That is why I ruffed high to prevent an overruff. You did not see the high-low in hearts?'

Sam waved his hand dismissively. 'A high-low from the Rabbi is like a low-high from anyone else,' he declared. 'It would not have fooled me, let me tell you.'

The Rabbi smiled. 'Perhaps you were right first time, Sam,' he said. 'Three No-trumps would have been cold.'

So would Four Spades played by me, thought Sam.

Both sides scored a game, then this deal arose:

Game all
Dealer South

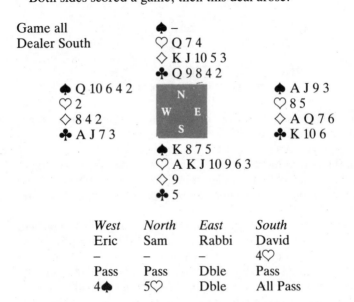

♠ –
♥ Q 7 4
♦ K J 10 5 3
♣ Q 9 8 4 2

♠ Q 10 6 4 2
♥ 2
♦ 8 4 2
♣ A J 7 3

♠ A J 9 3
♥ 8 5
♦ A Q 7 6
♣ K 10 6

♠ K 8 7 5
♥ A K J 10 9 6 3
♦ 9
♣ 5

West	North	East	South
Eric	Sam	Rabbi	David
–	–	–	4♡
Pass	Pass	Dble	Pass
4♠	5♡	Dble	All Pass

The Rabbi's initial double showed a strong hand ('strength is in the eye of the beholder,' he was wont to say). The call served its purpose when Sam took the push to the five level. Eric knew what to lead after such an auction. He flipped a trump on to the table and David won in the South hand. Since he would now be restricted to only one spade ruff, he decided to make something of the diamonds. At trick two he led ♢9, running the card.

Before playing to this trick, the Rabbi paused for thought. Eric's 2 proclaimed three cards in the suit, giving declarer a singleton. If he won the trick with the queen, declarer would be able to cross to dummy with a trump and take a ruffing finesse through the diamond ace. He could then use dummy's remaining trump entry to enjoy three discards on the diamond suit.

How to defend? Perhaps he could win with the ace, pretending that Eric held the queen. Declarer would have one discard on the diamond king but might then try to ruff out the queen instead of taking a ruffing finesse.

A better idea occurred to the Rabbi. He allowed ♢9 to win! Declarer now had no way to make the contract. He scored two spade ruffs but eventually lost one club and two spades.

'One down?' queried Sam.

'Yes, but what a shame you bid Five Hearts,' replied David. 'I set them a clever trap with my Four Hearts. I was hoping they would go to Four Spades, so I could double. I had four trumps to the king.'

Sam drew breath to make some caustic reply but the Rabbi intervened. 'Is it true that you made out a new will at the weekend, Sam?' he asked.

'I did, as a matter of fact,' replied Sam. 'No easy task these days, with so many hoping for something.'

'You looked kindly on your son, Warren?' enquired the Rabbi. 'I know you don't approve of his lifestyle but blood is blood, as they say.'

'In the circumstances I was very generous, believe me,' declared Sam. 'I left him all the money he owes me. Every penny of it.'

Not long afterwards David had another chance to win the rubber.

Game all
Dealer East

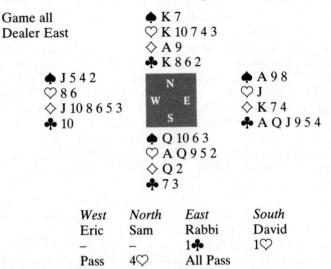

♠ K 7
♡ K 10 7 4 3
♢ A 9
♣ K 8 6 2

♠ J 5 4 2
♡ 8 6
♢ J 10 8 6 5 3
♣ 10

♠ A 9 8
♡ J
♢ K 7 4
♣ A Q J 9 5 4

♠ Q 10 6 3
♡ A Q 9 5 2
♢ Q 2
♣ 7 3

West	*North*	*East*	*South*
Eric	Sam	Rabbi	David
–	–	1♣	1♡
Pass	4♡	All Pass	

Eric led ♣10 and down went the dummy. 'King, please,' said David.

Sam shrugged his shoulders as the king lost to the ace. 'You thought Eric had underled the club ace?' he said. 'The Rabbi opened One Club.'

The Rabbi cashed a second round of clubs, West discarding a diamond. He continued with a third high club, David ruffing with the ace. A trump to the king dropped the Rabbi's jack. David ruffed dummy's last club with the queen and returned to dummy with a trump to the 10. What to play next? Perhaps he should lead a low spade. Yes, if the Rabbi went in with the ace there would be a discard for dummy's diamond loser.

When David led a low spade from the dummy the Rabbi played low. Declarer's queen won the trick and he continued with a spade to the king and ace. The Rabbi was on lead in this end position:

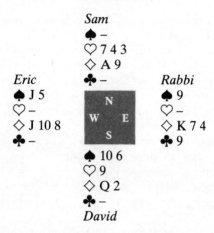

Sam
♠ –
♡ 7 4 3
♢ A 9
♣ –

Eric
♠ J 5
♡ –
♢ J 10 8
♣ –

Rabbi
♠ 9
♡ –
♢ K 7 4
♣ 9

David
♠ 10 6
♡ 9
♢ Q 2
♣ –

The Rabbi could not play a diamond from the king; nor a club, which would concede a ruff-and-discard. He exited with ♠9, covered by the 10 and jack. A dispirited David ruffed in the dummy and crossed to his hand with a trump to the 9. It seemed that Sam would be cross again. He could ruff the small spade but the eventual diamond loser would mean one down.

When David led ♣6 a miracle occurred. West could only produce the 5! David stared at this card in disbelief. Yes, it was definitely the 5. He discarded a diamond from dummy and a few seconds later had ten tricks stacked before him.

'Brilliant play, David!' congratulated the Rabbi. 'The key moment was at trick 1, I think, when you covered the club lead with the king. If you duck, Eric can hold the lead and switch to a diamond.'

David surveyed the scene with a dazed expression. 'That's just what I thought,' he said.

'Very nice play indeed, David,' observed Eric. 'For a moment the Rabbi must have thought he was playing against himself.'

'Shall we take a break?' suggested the Rabbi.

The players moved to the next room and the Rabbi soon returned with a pot of extra-strong coffee.

'I forgot to mention some good news, Rabbi,' said Eric. 'We are about to receive a big donation for the Shule.'

The Rabbi nodded enthusiastically. 'From whom and how much?' he asked.

'Ten thousand pounds, no less,' replied Eric. 'From Ira Levine.'

Sam was unimpressed. 'Believe it when you have it in your hand,' he said. 'Anyone more tight-fisted than Ira, I have yet to meet.'

'No, it's true,' declared Eric. 'The Tax Office phoned him to check his tax relief claim for the donation.'

Sam laughed. 'Now you make more sense!' he exclaimed. 'He has actually made the donation, then?'

'Well, not physically,' replied Eric. 'But I feel sure he is about to.'

'I once visited Ira in hospital when he was recovering from an operation,' said Sam. 'I told him the Board had voted 10–8 in favour of wishing him a speedy recovery.'

'You didn't!' exclaimed the Rabbi.

'No,' admitted Sam. 'But I was tempted.'

The players returned to the card table for the final rubber of the evening. On the first hand Sam arrived in 3NT.

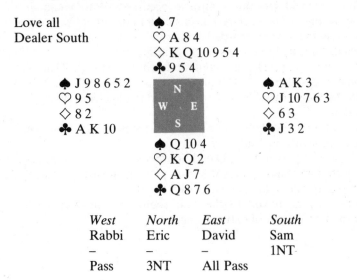

Love all
Dealer South

North
♠ 7
♡ A 8 4
◇ K Q 10 9 5 4
♣ 9 5 4

West
♠ J 9 8 6 5 2
♡ 9 5
◇ 8 2
♣ A K 10

East
♠ A K 3
♡ J 10 7 6 3
◇ 6 3
♣ J 3 2

South
♠ Q 10 4
♡ K Q 2
◇ A J 7
♣ Q 8 7 6

West	North	East	South
Rabbi	Eric	David	Sam
–	–	–	1NT
Pass	3NT	All Pass	

The Rabbi led ♠6 against 3NT and David won with the king. When he continued with the ace of spades, South followed with the 10. The Rabbi paused to consider the situation. South was marked with the spade queen and surely had at least eight tricks ready to run in the red suits. How could he dissuade David from a fatal spade continuation?

The Rabbi soon came up with the answer. Under his partner's ace of spades he played the jack, an informative card which denied the queen. With three small clubs visible in the dummy, David would surely try his luck in that quarter.

'You were worried I did not have another spade?' said David, smiling at the Rabbi as he continued with a third spade.

Sam faced his hand, claiming ten tricks.

'No,' replied the Rabbi. 'I was *hoping* you did not have another spade.'

Sam stared at David as if he were some lowly form of life. 'The Rabbi played the jack of spades,' he said. 'It was obvious to switch to clubs.'

'I play any card above the 6 as encouraging,' protested David. 'If a jack isn't an encouraging card, I don't know what is.'

'Before I forget, Rabbi, I have a joke for you,' said Eric. 'A bus driver in Jerusalem is distracted by a pretty girl walking at the side of the road and drives straight into the back of a lorry that has stopped ahead. You have heard it?'

'No,' replied the Rabbi.

'There are four passengers on the bus and they all suffer whip-lash injuries,' said Eric. 'Before two minutes have passed Shmuel Cohen, a lawyer, is on the scene to represent them.'

The Rabbi smiled. 'Bad news for some is good news for others,' he observed.

Eric continued the story. 'The bus driver says to Shmuel: you are going to represent all four passengers yourself? The lawyer looks surprised. What do you mean, four? he says. By the time I arrived there were *twelve* in the bus complaining of whiplash!'

'Twelve complaining, very good,' said the Rabbi. 'And all too typical of how people look for something out of nothing nowadays.'

A hand or so later, with Sam and Eric now a game ahead, the Rabbi picked up this hand:

♠ A K J 9 3 2   ♡ Q 5 2   ◇ A 4   ♣ 4 3

Not the world's worst hand. If David had the odd card or two, game should be there. 'One Spade,' said Sam, to the Rabbi's right.

Just what I wanted to hear, thought the Rabbi. 'No bid.'

Eric responded Two Clubs, on the Rabbi's left, then raised the 2NT rebid to 3NT. As the Rabbi had foreseen, game had been reached. Unfortunately by the other side. Now, what to lead?

There was something to be said for a passive lead, hoping that the bad lie of the spade suit would be enough to put the contract down. This was not the Rabbi's style. With a purposeful air he reached for a card that would not have occurred to many players – the queen of hearts. This was the full deal:

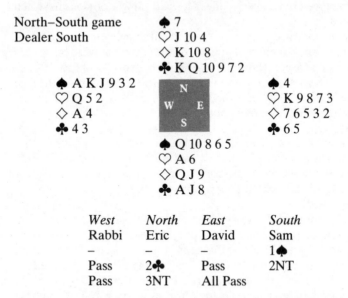

North–South game   ♠ 7
Dealer South   ♡ J 10 4
                        ◇ K 10 8
                        ♣ K Q 10 9 7 2

♠ A K J 9 3 2   ♠ 4
♡ Q 5 2   N   ♡ K 9 8 7 3
◇ A 4   W   E   ◇ 7 6 5 3 2
♣ 4 3   S   ♣ 6 5

                        ♠ Q 10 8 6 5
                        ♡ A 6
                        ◇ Q J 9
                        ♣ A J 8

West	North	East	South
Rabbi	Eric	David	Sam
–	–	–	1♠
Pass	2♣	Pass	2NT
Pass	3NT	All Pass	

David signalled enthusiastically with the 9 of hearts and Sam captured with the ace. When he played the queen of diamonds the

Rabbi won with the ace and played a second heart. The jack was played from dummy and David sat back in his chair, considering what to do. The Rabbi's elation at having found the killing lead began to drain. Put up the king, partner, and switch to a spade! Still David was looking at his hand. Eventually he played the 8 of hearts, allowing dummy's jack to win.

Sam looked disdainfully at David. 'Ten tricks,' he said, facing his hand.

David gave a disappointed shake of the head. 'My clever play in hearts went unrewarded,' he declared. 'Ducking to preserve communications. I rarely spot such plays in time.'

Sam laughed. 'It was my lucky day that you managed to spot it this time,' he observed. 'Win and switch to a spade and I have had it.'

'Switch to declarer's suit, is that how to defend?,' exclaimed David. 'Only an idiot would defend this way.'

Or someone who can count nine tricks for declarer in the other three suits, thought the Rabbi.

The players settled for the final rubber, then rose to their feet. 'An enjoyable session, as always,' said Eric. 'Can I offer you a lift home, David? It is not much out of my way.'

'No need, thanks very much,' replied David. 'I am always happy to take a taxi.'

5.   The Commemoration of St Benedict

'Rabbi, do you know what year St Benedict died?' asked Sam, who had an open letter in his hand.

'I could hazard a guess,' replied the Rabbi. 'There's not much point, however. I've never heard of the gentleman.'

'He died exactly 500 years ago next Friday,' said Sam. 'I have a letter here from Father O'Ryan at St Benedict's Church, across town. As part of the celebrations for this anniversary, he asks us to play their team in a small match.'

'On Shabbat?' exclaimed the Rabbi. 'Impossible.'

'Yes, yes, he knows that,' continued Sam. 'He suggests the day before, the Thursday.'

'Well, in that case why not?' replied the Rabbi. 'In this day and age we must make an effort to communicate with the other denominations.'

The following Thursday the Rabbi's team arrived at the small hall behind St Benedict's Church. The Rabbi would partner Sam, with Miriam and the Cantor at the other table.

'Welcome, welcome,' declared Father O'Ryan. 'The tables are set up in here. You don't mind a few spectators, I trust?'

The Cantor blanched at the sight before him. At least twenty spectators surrounded each table. Had they told him that when he agreed to play?

The first half of the match saw Sam and the Rabbi playing against two Catholic priests, Father O'Ryan and his rather over-weight partner, Father Grierson.

'Nice day for the match, Rabbi,' observed Father O'Ryan. 'According to church records, it was a similarly sunny day 500 years ago, when the blessed St Benedict died.'

Father Grierson crossed himself. 'Let us hope it is a good omen, Father,' he declared.

With the kibitzers pressing forward to obtain a good view, the players drew their cards for the first board of the match.

Game all   ♠ K J 8 5
Dealer South   ♡ –
                            ◇ K 6 5
                            ♣ Q 10 9 7 5 3

♠ 10 6 2   ♠ 9 4 3
♡ A K 10 6 4 3   N   ♡ Q J 5
◇ 7   W   E   ◇ Q 9 3
♣ A J 8   S   ♣ K 6 4 2

                            ♠ A Q 7
                            ♡ 9 8 7 2
                            ◇ A J 10 8 4 2
                            ♣ –

West	North	East	South
Father	Sam	Father	The
O'Ryan		Grierson	Rabbi
–	–	–	1◇
2♡	Dble	Pass	3◇
Pass	4♡	Dble	4♠
Pass	5◇	Pass	6◇
All Pass			

Father O'Ryan led the ace of hearts and was disappointed to see a void heart appear in the dummy. He looked at Sam with a puzzled expression. 'How can you double Two Hearts?' he demanded.

'It was a negative double,' replied Sam.

'Negative double?' exclaimed the priest. 'How absurd. It's turning bridge on its head if you double with no trumps at all.'

'Yes, very sharp,' added the plump Father Grierson. 'I would have raised the hearts if I'd known.'

Sam looked back uncertainly. Were they trying to be funny or was their experience restricted to rubber bridge? 'My partner did alert the bid,' he replied.

'And what in Heaven's name was this Four Hearts?' demanded Father O'Ryan. 'Were you trying to make fun of us?'

'It was a splinter bid,' replied Sam. 'It shows at most one heart.'

'Would that be a Jewish convention?' queried Father O'Ryan. 'Stayman and Blackwood I know, but the man Splinter is a stranger to me.'

Unsure what to make of this pantomime, the Rabbi turned his mind to the play. He ruffed the heart lead, crossed to his hand with the ace of spades, and ruffed a second heart.

A club ruff to hand permitted a third heart ruff with the king. The Rabbi returned to his hand with a second club ruff and continued with the ace and jack of trumps. West showed out on the second round and East won with the queen. As the Rabbi had expected, he had no heart to return. When he played a club, the Rabbi ruffed and proceeded to draw East's last trump. He discarded his last heart on the fourth round of spades and that was twelve tricks.

'Twenty points to each side and they make a slam,' exclaimed Father O'Ryan. 'It's a miracle and that's the truth. Should have been a part-score deal with the points divided like that.'

'Lead a trump, Father,' said Father Grierson. 'You stop him taking so many ruffs.'

Yes, thought the Rabbi. Provided East retained his queen of trumps at trick 1, the contract would then go down. If declarer took two heart ruffs with the 6 and king, East's trump queen would be revived.

'When you doubled Four Hearts I thought you wanted a heart lead,' retorted Father O'Ryan. 'Without the double I might well have led a trump.'

'My double of Four Hearts was a penalty double, Father,' replied Father Grierson. 'I don't play these Negative Doubles. I've never heard of them.'

Meanwhile Miriam and the Cantor found themselves facing a couple of aged nuns. Much to their surprise, the nuns' computer-generated convention card ran to several pages and included all the latest methods.

Love all
Dealer South

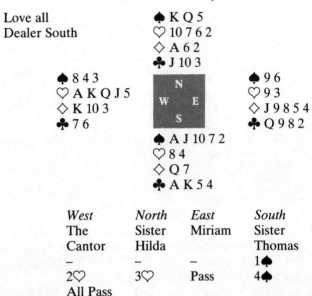

```
              ♠ K Q 5
              ♡ 10 7 6 2
              ◇ A 6 2
              ♣ J 10 3
♠ 8 4 3                        ♠ 9 6
♡ A K Q J 5         N          ♡ 9 3
◇ K 10 3       W        E      ◇ J 9 8 5 4
♣ 7 6              S           ♣ Q 9 8 2
              ♠ A J 10 7 2
              ♡ 8 4
              ◇ Q 7
              ♣ A K 5 4
```

West	North	East	South
The	Sister	Miriam	Sister
Cantor	Hilda		Thomas
–	–	–	1♠
2♡	3♡	Pass	4♠
All Pass			

'You alerted the Three Heart bid?' queried the Cantor, who was on lead.

The ancient Sister Thomas peered at him from beneath her wimple. 'It shows a sound raise with only 3-card trump support,' she replied, speaking very slowly. 'With four trumps and a sound raise the Sister would have bid 2NT.'

Miriam and the Cantor shared a glance. Contrary to appearances, these opponents might be no push-over.

The Cantor cashed two top hearts successfully and continued with the heart queen. Sister Thomas ruffed in the South hand and drew trumps in three rounds, ending in the dummy. The jack of clubs was run successfully and she continued with the ace and king of clubs, West showing out on the third round. Declarer cashed her last trump, leaving these cards still to be played:

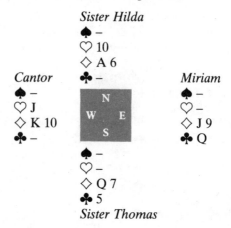

Sister Hilda
♠ –
♡ 10
♢ A 6
♣ –

Cantor
♠ –
♡ J
♢ K 10
♣ –

Miriam
♠ –
♡ –
♢ J 9
♣ Q

♠ –
♡ –
♢ Q 7
♣ 5

Sister Thomas

With a purposeful air the ancient nun placed her last club on to the table. Not liking the situation too much, the Cantor discarded ♢10. 'Heart away, Sister,' said Sister Thomas.

Miriam won the trick and returned a diamond but Sister Thomas did not hesitate with her play. She contributed ♢7 from her hand and claimed the contract when West's king appeared.

'Did you make it?' asked a bald-headed kibitzer.

The nun gave a small nod of the head.

'She made it, everyone!' cried the kibitzer, leading a round of applause.

Miriam and the Cantor made little headway on the remaining boards of the first half and soon rejoined the Rabbi to compare scores.

'One-way traffic, it was rather embarrassing,' declared the Rabbi. 'The same in your room?'

The Cantor was looking somewhat shell-shocked. 'One-way traffic, yes,' he replied. 'But not in our direction. They played us off the park.'

The Rabbi could hardly believe it when his side proved to be only 2 IMPs in the lead. In the second half it was his turn to face the two ancient nuns. He eyed them curiously as the players drew their cards for the first board.

East–West game
Dealer West

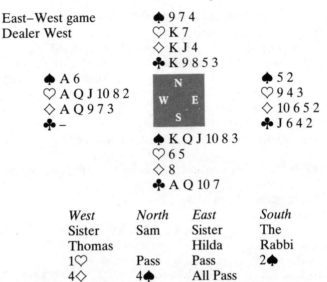

```
                    ♠ 9 7 4
                    ♡ K 7
                    ♢ K J 4
                    ♣ K 9 8 5 3
♠ A 6                               ♠ 5 2
♡ A Q J 10 8 2        N             ♡ 9 4 3
♢ A Q 9 7 3      W        E         ♢ 10 6 5 2
♣ –                  S             ♣ J 6 4 2
                    ♠ K Q J 10 8 3
                    ♡ 6 5
                    ♢ 8
                    ♣ A Q 10 7
```

West	North	East	South
Sister	Sam	Sister	The
Thomas		Hilda	Rabbi
1♡	Pass	Pass	2♠
4♢	4♠	All Pass	

When the opponents reached Four Spades Sister Thomas decided not to press any further on her fine hand. With her eye on a possible club ruff, she selected ♡2 as her opening lead. 'King, please,' said the Rabbi.

The king of hearts won the first trick and the Rabbi turned immediately to the trump suit. Sister Thomas won the first round with the ace and paused to consider her continuation. Had her partner played a high heart on the first round, ace and another heart at this stage might have led to an overruff. East's actual 3 on the first round of hearts suggested three cards in the suit. In that case, thought Sister Thomas, the odds were 3-to-2 in favour of her holding ♡9.

At trick 3 the aged nun in the West seat played ♡8. East overtook with the 9 and gave her partner a club ruff. Sister Thomas was not slow to place her ace of diamonds on the table and the Rabbi was one down.

There was prolonged applause from the kibitzers. 'A defence to impress St Benedict himself, Sister,' declared a man in a home-made pullover.

A woman nearby chuckled to herself. 'Not to mention our Treasurer, of course,' she added.

The Rabbi looked round. 'The treasurer?' he queried.

'I was thinking of the prize money for the match,' replied the woman, 'should the Lord choose to look fondly on the side representing St Benedict's.'

The Rabbi leaned towards Sam. 'Was there any mention of prize money?' he asked.

'Not that I know,' replied Sam. 'Perhaps I didn't read the whole letter.'

At the other table Miriam and the Cantor faced the two priests.

North–South game
Dealer East

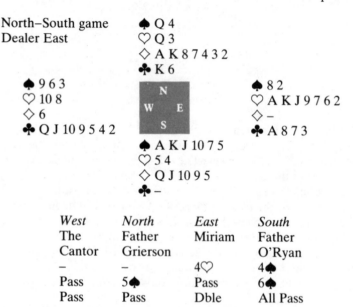

	♠ Q 4	
	♡ Q 3	
	♢ A K 8 7 4 3 2	
	♣ K 6	
♠ 9 6 3		♠ 8 2
♡ 10 8		♡ A K J 9 7 6 2
♢ 6		♢ –
♣ Q J 10 9 5 4 2		♣ A 8 7 3
	♠ A K J 10 7 5	
	♡ 5 4	
	♢ Q J 10 9 5	
	♣ –	

West	North	East	South
The	Father	Miriam	Father
Cantor	Grierson		O'Ryan
–	–	4♡	4♠
Pass	5♠	Pass	6♠
Pass	Pass	Dble	All Pass

Miriam opened Four Hearts and was surprised to find the priests in Six Spades a few moments later. No doubt one of them held a void heart. Still, so long as Michael led a diamond, the contract would go at least one down. 'Double,' she said.

There was no further bidding. Miriam raised an alarmed eyebrow when the Cantor led the queen of clubs rather than the required diamond. Had Michael forgotten what it meant, when she doubled a freely bid slam? Still, with K x in the dummy it might not work so badly.

'They're all there, I think,' said Father O'Ryan, displaying his hand. 'I can ruff the lead. Then I make five more trumps and seven diamonds.'

There was a burst of applause from the kibitzers. 'St Benedict be praised!' exclaimed a woman in a blue hat. 'Five hundred years to the day. I'm sure he intervened on that one.'

'It may have been more a question of luck,' declared Father Grierson. 'I intended my Five Spades to ask for a heart control.'

'A heart control?' exclaimed his partner. 'What nonsense, five of a major asks for good trumps.' He turned to the kibitzers behind him. 'If A K J 10 to six trumps doesn't count as good, I don't know what does.'

'And you were doubled, too,' added one of the kibitzers. 'The Lord be praised! A doubled overtrick.'

Miriam gave the Cantor an anguished glance. 'It was a Lightner Double, Michael,' she said. 'You did not think to lead a diamond?'

The Cantor blinked. With seven clubs and one diamond he could know to give his partner a diamond ruff?

'A heart lead would beat it too,' observed Father O'Ryan. 'It usually pays to lead your partner's suit. Did you not hear the opening bid?'

Back at the other table the Rabbi had just arrived in Four Spades. This was the deal:

East–West game   ♠ Q J 7 3
Dealer South   ♡ Q 9 6 4
                        ◇ 7 5 3
                        ♣ Q J

♠ 8 6 2   ♠ K
♡ A K J 10 8 5 3   ♡ 2
◇ Q J 4   ◇ A 9 2
♣ –   ♣ 10 9 8 6 5 4 3 2

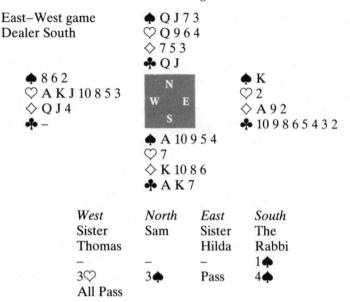

                        ♠ A 10 9 5 4
                        ♡ 7
                        ◇ K 10 8 6
                        ♣ A K 7

West	North	East	South
Sister	Sam	Sister	The
Thomas		Hilda	Rabbi
–	–	–	1♠
3♡	3♠	Pass	4♠
All Pass			

Sister Thomas led the ace of hearts, then switched to the queen of diamonds. East won with the ace and all depended on her choice of return. Sister Hilda paused to construct the hidden hands. The Rabbi surely held the ace and king of clubs to make up his opening bid. If he held ♣A K doubleton, Sister Thomas would hold a singleton club. She would surely have switched to it in that case. Yes, the position was clear. West must hold a void club.

The kibitzers behind Sister Hilda were surprised to see her return, not a club, but a second round of diamonds. The Rabbi won with the king and crossed to dummy's queen of clubs to take a trump finesse. That was his intention, at any rate. In fact West pounced with a trump and cashed a diamond trick. The contract was one down.

'Well defended, Sister,' observed Sister Thomas, having to shout over the applause from the kibitzers. 'Give me a club ruff and he cannot fail to make it.'

'Of course, Sister,' her partner shouted back. 'He's forced to drop my king of trumps and dummy's diamond loser goes on the third club.'

The final comparison was not even close. The St Benedict's team had won by a full 23 IMPs.

'Thank you for the game,' declared the two nuns, poking their heads around the door. 'We're back off to Manchester now.'

The Rabbi waved a farewell and turned to Father O'Ryan. 'They come from Manchester?' he exclaimed.

'Yes,' replied the priest. 'Apart from Father Grierson and myself none of our local players are any good at all.'

'We put an advertisement in the *Catholic Herald*,' said Father Grierson. 'For Grandmasters they were very reasonable.'

'It was on a "no win, no fee" basis,' continued Father O'Ryan, 'and, being for a good cause, they only charged half the normal amount.'

'Their generosity was much appreciated,' declared Father Grierson. 'As will be your own contribution to the St Benedict's fund. We did agree 500 pounds to the winners, didn't we?'

With a hint of embarrassment the Rabbi beckoned to Sam. 'Can you do the necessary?' he said. 'We can sort it out later.'

Sam reached reluctantly for his wallet. 'You take American Express, Father?' he said.

The priest nodded happily. 'That will do nicely,' he said.

6. Alan Neufeld's Bridge Barmitzvah

'Ah, Rabbi,' said Mitzi Neufeld. 'I have a small favour to ask you. Please say you will do it.'

'I like to help where I can,' replied the Rabbi cheerfully. 'What favour is it?'

'No, no, say you will do it first,' persisted Mitzi Neufeld. 'Then I will tell you.'

The Rabbi laughed. 'Some people I would not trust so much,' he observed. 'All right, I will do it. Now tell me what it is I must do.'

Mitzi gazed triumphantly at her husband, by her side. 'You see, Ronnie?' she said. 'I told you he would agree.'

An embarrassed Ronald Neufeld shrugged his shoulders.

'Our young Alan is learning bridge with Heidi Levine,' continued Mitzi. 'She says he is promising, very promising for his age.'

Would she never get to the point, thought Ronald Neufeld.

'We would like you to come to supper and make up a four afterwards,' continued Mitzi Neufeld. 'Then you can tell us your honest opinion, what you think of young Alan's game.'

'Come to supper?' said the Rabbi. 'I wish I could grant such favours every night. I look forward to it.'

The following Thursday Mitzi producing a supper fit for a king. Or fit for a Chief Rabbi, perhaps one should say.

'The chopped liver is from Blumenthal's,' declared Mitzi proudly. 'It is a favourite of yours, Rabbi, I know.'

'So it is,' declared the Rabbi appreciatively. 'Such a long way to go for it.'

'Only a 45-minute drive,' replied Mitzi. 'Ronnie was pleased to do it.'

The Rabbi felt he was some five pounds heavier as they moved into the Neufelds' elegant drawing room for a few rubbers. The Rabbi cut to partner Mrs Neufeld and this was the first deal:

Love all   ♠ K J 10
Dealer South   ♡ K 5 2
                ◇ 10 8 4 3
                ♣ Q 5 2

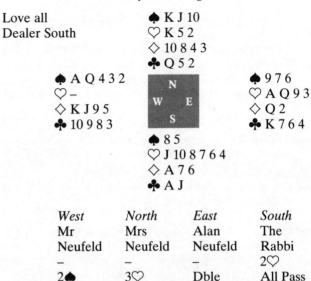

♠ A Q 4 3 2   ♠ 9 7 6
♡ –   ♡ A Q 9 3
◇ K J 9 5   ◇ Q 2
♣ 10 9 8 3   ♣ K 7 6 4

                ♠ 8 5
                ♡ J 10 8 7 6 4
                ◇ A 7 6
                ♣ A J

West	*North*	*East*	*South*
Mr	Mrs	Alan	The
Neufeld	Neufeld	Neufeld	Rabbi
–	–	–	2♡
2♠	3♡	Dble	All Pass

Not exactly happy with the path the auction had taken, Mr Neufeld led ♣10. The Rabbi won with the jack and played back a spade. Mr Neufeld rose with the ace and switched promptly to diamonds, East's queen forcing the ace. The Rabbi finessed successfully in spades, then played the king of spades. East followed suit and he discarded one of his diamond losers.

So, thought the Rabbi, young Alan has doubled me when he holds three-card spade support. That must mean he holds all four trumps. The Rabbi led the 2 of trumps from the dummy and East contributed the 3.

'Cover an honour with an honour, they say,' observed the Rabbi. 'Perhaps there is a similar rule for low spot-cards.'

The Rabbi produced the 4 of trumps and Mr Neufeld discarded a spade. There was nothing further to the play. The Rabbi conceded two trump tricks, one spade and one diamond, making his contract.

Mr Neufeld glared at his chubby, 15-year-old son. 'I pay five pounds a lesson for this?' he exclaimed. 'You think, on the very first hand, it is a good idea to double them into game?'

'How did I know you would make such a lead?' replied his son.

'There was nothing wrong with the double. Lead a diamond and it is one down.'

'Don't speak to your father like that!' said Mrs Neufeld.

Mr Neufeld glared at his son. 'Heidi Levine teaches you to lead from kings?' he demanded. 'No good player would dream of such a lead. When you have played bridge as long as I have, you will know that.'

Soon afterwards the Rabbi had a chance to win the first rubber. He reached 6NT on this deal:

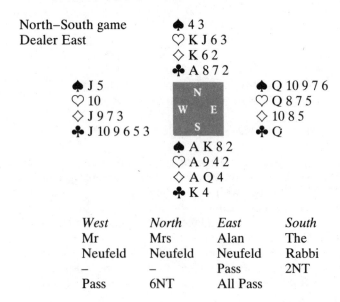

North–South game   ♠ 4 3
Dealer East   ♡ K J 6 3
                    ◇ K 6 2
                    ♣ A 8 7 2

♠ J 5   ♠ Q 10 9 7 6
♡ 10   N   ♡ Q 8 7 5
◇ J 9 7 3   W   E   ◇ 10 8 5
♣ J 10 9 6 5 3   S   ♣ Q

                    ♠ A K 8 2
                    ♡ A 9 4 2
                    ◇ A Q 4
                    ♣ K 4

West	North	East	South
Mr	Mrs	Alan	The
Neufeld	Neufeld	Neufeld	Rabbi
–	–	Pass	2NT
Pass	6NT	All Pass	

The ♣J was led against 6NT and Mrs Neufeld laid out her dummy. 'I never know on these hands, Rabbi,' she said. 'To Stayman or not to Stayman?'

The Rabbi surveyed the dummy. Only 11 points facing a 2NT opening? A better question would be: to bid slam or not to bid slam?

The Rabbi won the club lead with the king, noting the fall of the queen from East. When he returned a second round of clubs Mr Neufeld considered the matter for a moment, then split his 10 9. The Rabbi won in the dummy and cleared an extra trick for himself in clubs. Mr Neufeld won with the 9 and exited safely with his last club. The Rabbi discarded a spade and a diamond. Alan Neufeld threw a spade and two diamonds.

The Rabbi now cashed the ace and queen of diamonds. When East showed out on the second diamond, having already thrown two diamonds, the count was nearly complete. The Rabbi continued with the spade ace–king, discovering that West's shape was 2–1–4–6. No future in finessing the heart jack, then!

The Rabbi played a heart to dummy's king, pleased to see the 10 appear from West. These cards remained:

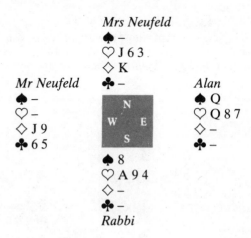

```
                        Mrs Neufeld
                        ♠ –
                        ♡ J 6 3
                        ◇ K
        Mr Neufeld      ♣ –              Alan
        ♠ –                              ♠ Q
        ♡ –             N                ♡ Q 8 7
        ◇ J 9        W     E             ◇ –
        ♣ 6 5           S                ♣ –
                        ♠ 8
                        ♡ A 9 4
                        ◇ –
                        ♣ –
                        Rabbi
```

The king of diamonds forced a heart discard from Alan. The Rabbi threw ♠8 and proceeded to finesse ♡9, claiming the contract.

'What a lead again!' exclaimed Alan Neufeld. 'You killed my queen of clubs.'

'Don't be silly, Alan,' retorted Mrs Neufeld. 'Everyone in the world would lead a club from J 10 9. The lesson of the hand was in my bidding. Isn't that so, Rabbi?'

The Rabbi, with no idea what she meant, nodded politely.

'Most people would Stayman on my hand and end in Six Hearts,' continued Mrs Neufeld. 'No chance at all when the trumps break 4–1.'

Mr Neufeld left the table briefly to open a bottle of South African Merlot. He returned with three generously filled glasses.

'No wine for me?' queried Alan Neufeld.

'What a question!' exclaimed his father. 'Only 15 and you would drink alcohol before your Rabbi?'

'Don't worry on my account,' said the Rabbi.

'Alan, get your homework book while we have this wine,' said Mrs Neufeld. 'The Rabbi would like to see what good marks you have been getting.'

'Which one?' said Alan sullenly. 'The one for French?'

'You think the Rabbi wants to look at a C+ on every page?' his mother exclaimed. 'No, the one for economics. That is the one he would like to see.'

The Rabbi made suitable noises as he leafed through the exercise book. 'Your parents must be very proud of you, Alan,' he said.

The game had only just restarted when Mr Neufeld arrived in a slam.

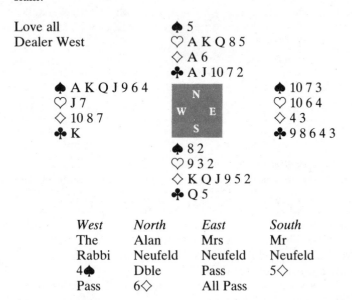

Love all
Dealer West

♠ 5
♡ A K Q 8 5
◇ A 6
♣ A J 10 7 2

♠ A K Q J 9 6 4
♡ J 7
◇ 10 8 7
♣ K

♠ 10 7 3
♡ 10 6 4
◇ 4 3
♣ 9 8 6 4 3

♠ 8 2
♡ 9 3 2
◇ K Q J 9 5 2
♣ Q 5

West	North	East	South
The	Alan	Mrs	Mr
Rabbi	Neufeld	Neufeld	Neufeld
4♠	Dble	Pass	5◇
Pass	6◇	All Pass	

The Rabbi led the ace of spades and down went the dummy.

'You are drunk, Alan?' exclaimed Mr Neufeld. 'You go to six on your own hand with only 18 points and ace–one support?'

'How can I be drunk when you wouldn't let me have any wine?'

retorted his son. 'When you pulled my double I put you with a good suit.'

Mr Neufeld shook his head. 'Such ideas that Heidi puts into his head,' he muttered. 'I should pay five pounds an hour for this?'

At trick 2 the Rabbi continued with the king of spades, attacking dummy's trump holding. Mr Neufeld was about to ruff with the 6 when he saw that the trump suit would then be blocked. After cashing the ace, he would have no entry to his hand to draw the remaining trumps. 'Ruff with the ace,' he said.

Now, thought Mr Neufeld, how would the trump suit lie? The Rabbi must hold seven spades, maybe eight. Surely Mitzi was favourite to hold the 10 of trumps. Perhaps in a 4-card holding, too. Yes, the percentage play was to finesse the trump 9.

Mr Neufeld played a trump to the 9 and the Rabbi won somewhat apologetically with the 10. The king of clubs now locked declarer in the dummy. He had to try a club to the queen and the Rabbi ruffed for a second time, putting the slam two down.

'You could make it!' exclaimed Alan Neufeld. 'Just play trumps from the top and you have twelve tricks.'

'Don't speak to your father like that,' cried Mitzi Neufeld. 'He must have a reason for playing it in that strange way.'

'Of course I must play East for the trump length,' said Mr Neufeld. 'We shouldn't be in Six Diamonds. That was the problem.'

'What difference would it make?' replied his son. 'You didn't even make five.'

Mitzi Neufeld gazed at her son with mixed feelings. 'Only 15 and he plays already like a grown-up player,' she observed. 'He is even as rude as a grown-up player.'

'In my day a child would be smacked for such rudeness,' declared Mr Neufeld. 'Nowadays they send parents to jail for such things.'

The final rubber of the evening saw Alan Neufeld in partnership with his mother. The youngster reached a grand slam, no less, on this deal:

Love all   ♠ –
Dealer South   ♡ A K Q 6
                                 ◇ K Q 9
                                 ♣ A K 9 7 5 4

♠ 10 9 8 7 6 5 2   N   ♠ K 3
♡ 9 7   W   E   ♡ J 10 5 2
◇ 10 7 2   S   ◇ J 4
♣ 6   ♣ Q J 8 3 2

                                 ♠ A Q J 4
                                 ♡ 8 4 3
                                 ◇ A 8 6 5 3
                                 ♣ 10

West	North	East	South
Mr	Mrs	The	Alan
Neufeld	Neufeld	Rabbi	Neufeld
–	–	–	1◇
Pass	3♣	Pass	3◇
Pass	7◇	All Pass	

West led ♠10 against Seven Diamonds. 'Such a hand I have for you!' exclaimed Mrs Neufeld. 'You will claim the contract at trick 1.'

The youngster reached forward to discard a club from dummy.

'You don't say thank you to your Mother for a dummy like that?' exclaimed Mr Neufeld. 'In my day we said a thank you when the dummy had only two jacks.'

Meanwhile, the Rabbi was doing some quick thinking in the East seat. There were 21 points in the dummy and he had 8 points himself. Declarer must hold all the remaining points, including ♠A Q J. His calculations complete, the Rabbi contributed the 3 of spades to the first trick.

Alan Neufeld won with the spade queen. Provided the trumps broke 3–2 he could count five trump tricks and seven side-suit winners. If clubs were 4–2 or better he would be able to set up the suit with two ruffs. But in that case he could score a thirteenth trick simply by ruffing a spade, cashing the trump king–queen, then returning to his hand with a club ruff. That was a better line, in fact, because it would succeed also if clubs were 5–1 and East held the singleton club.

His mind made up, Alan ruffed ♠4 at trick 2, surprised to see the king fall from the Rabbi. He continued with the king and queen of trumps, both defenders following, then attempted to return to his hand with a club ruff. His mouth fell open when Mr Neufeld overruffed him with the 10. The slam was one down.

'You went down?' exclaimed Mrs Neufeld. 'With the dummy I gave you, you went down?'

Alan Neufeld glared accusingly at the Rabbi. 'He made it difficult,' he declared. 'If he plays the king of spades at trick 1, it is easy.'

'Don't make excuses for your poor play,' declared Mr Neufeld. 'You should cash the spade ace before taking the ruff. The king falls and you are home. Isn't that so, Rabbi?'

For once Neufeld is talking some sense, thought the Rabbi. He could support the parental authority without telling a white lie. 'Good point, Ronnie,' said the Rabbi. 'I was marked with the spade king, so no risk would be involved.'

A few deals later Alan Neufeld was declarer once more.

North–South game
Dealer South

```
                    ♠ A 6 4 3
                    ♡ J 3
                    ◇ A Q 6 3
                    ♣ Q 4 3
      ♠ 10 9 8           N              ♠ 7
      ♡ K 10 8 6 4    W     E           ♡ 9 7 5 2
      ◇ K 8                             ◇ 10 9 5 4
      ♣ J 7 6             S             ♣ 10 8 5 2
                    ♠ K Q J 5 2
                    ♡ A Q
                    ◇ J 7 2
                    ♣ A K 9
```

West	North	East	South
Mr	Mrs	The	Alan
Neufeld	Neufeld	Rabbi	Neufeld
–	–	–	1♠
Pass	4♠	Pass	4NT
Pass	5♡	Pass	6♠
All Pass			

The youngster arrived in Six Spades and Mr Neufeld led a trump. Alan Neufeld looked ahead to his play in the red suits. Suppose he played a diamond to the queen and this lost to the king. The Rabbi was sure to return a heart and he would then have to choose whether to finesse before he knew if the diamonds were 3–3. It must be better to lead a diamond towards the jack. If East went in with the king he would have three diamond tricks, enough for a heart discard. And if West won the jack with the king, or the jack held, he would be able to test for a 3–3 diamond break before falling back on a heart finesse.

Alan Neufeld drew trumps in two more rounds, ending in the dummy, then led a low diamond to the jack. Mr Neufeld won with the king and returned another diamond to dummy's ace. The diamonds failed to divide 3–3 and when the heart finesse lost too, the slam was one down.

'What a play he makes in diamonds here!' exclaimed Mr Neufeld. 'Finesse the queen, cash the ace, and my king would fall.'

'I still think my play was right,' declared Alan Neufeld. 'I was combining the chances.'

'Yes, combining the chance of making with the chance of going down,' replied Mr Neufeld. 'Let the Rabbi say who is right between us.'

The Rabbi smiled to himself. He would have played the hand in a different way. Draw trumps, eliminate clubs, then play ace and another diamond. It was a similar line to the young Alan's but would pick up the extra chance of end-playing West, should he hold king doubleton of diamonds. Still, this was not the time or place to expound such a line. In a Jewish family it is the parents who must rule the roost.

'Your father is right, Alan,' declared the Rabbi. 'Low to the jack was not the best idea.'

Mrs Neufeld looked gratefully at the Rabbi. 'It was so useful you coming over tonight,' she said. 'Alan thinks he is an expert already, but there is no substitute for experience in this game.'

'Quite right,' said Mr Neufeld. 'When you have played bridge as long as I have, you know what to do with an ace–queen in the dummy, believe me.'

7.   The Rabbi's Magic Trick

Sam's shoulders drooped as he inspected the results from the previous Thursday's pairs. 'Only fourteenth,' he said. 'What chance do I have, playing with that David?'

'Life is not meant to be easy,' replied the Rabbi. 'We must all make the best of what we are given.'

'Easy for you to say that, playing with Eric,' observed Sam. 'I'd like to see how you would cope with a useless partner.'

'Why don't we try it?' suggested the Rabbi. 'Next Thursday, in the pairs, I will play with David. You and Eric can play together.'

Sam brightened considerably. 'I will say a quick Yes before you change your mind,' he replied. 'But . . . how can I explain it to David?'

The Rabbi pondered the matter. 'Perhaps you could say that we are considering him for the synagogue first team,' he suggested, 'and I need to study his game.'

'If he believes that,' Sam replied, 'he is even more gullible than I thought.'

The following Thursday an excited David took his seat opposite the Rabbi. 'This is the system I play,' he said. 'I made a photo-copy of my convention card for you to use.'

'How kind of you,' replied the Rabbi. He looked at the mass of small print before him. 'You play the multi? Two Hearts and Two Spades are weak two-suiters with an unspecified minor, support doubles and redoubles, Lebensohl in all situations . . . Do you normally play all this?'

'No, but I have learnt it all for tonight,' replied David. 'I was reading a book on conventions until one in the morning, so I would not let you down.'

The first round of the event brought Jacob and Irene Kessler to the Rabbi's table. On the first hand Jacob opened with a weak Two Spades, showing 6–10 points. David doubled for take-out and Irene passed. The Rabbi looked down at this hand:

♠ K 7 2   ♡ 8 6 5   ◇ Q 10 4   ♣ K Q 3 2

David had written on the convention card 'Lebensohl in all situations'. Did that include when you were responding to a take-out of a Weak Two? If so, he would bid 2NT (a transfer to 3♣) on a hand of around 0–8 points, make a direct suit bid on an intermediate hand of around 9–11 points. Ah well, he would find out sooner or later. 'Three Clubs,' said the Rabbi.

David alerted the bid as conventional. 'Lebensohl convention', he said. 'It shows a good hand and a good suit.'

The Rabbi winced. A good suit? That was not part of the equation as he knew it.

Kessler passed and David inspected his hand learnedly. 'Six Clubs,' he said.

There was no further bidding. West led ◇2 and this was the full hand:

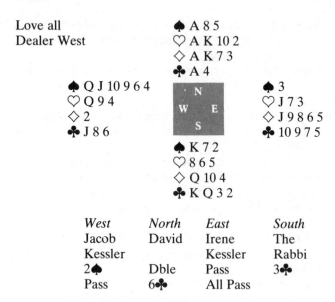

Love all
Dealer West

♠ A 8 5
♡ A K 10 2
◇ A K 7 3
♣ A 4

♠ Q J 10 9 6 4
♡ Q 9 4
◇ 2
♣ J 8 6

♠ 3
♡ J 7 3
◇ J 9 8 6 5
♣ 10 9 7 5

♠ K 7 2
♡ 8 6 5
◇ Q 10 4
♣ K Q 3 2

West	North	East	South
Jacob	David	Irene	The
Kessler		Kessler	Rabbi
2♠	Dble	Pass	3♣
Pass	6♣	All Pass	

'With my top cards facing your good suit, twelve tricks should be easy,' said David, as he put down the dummy.

The Rabbi won East's jack of diamonds with the queen and drew three rounds of trumps, pleased to see that they broke 4–3. A spade to the ace was followed by a spade towards the king. It would not help East to ruff a loser with her master trump. She discarded a heart and the Rabbi's king won the trick. Five red-suit winners followed in quick time, the Rabbi discarding his last spade. Eleven tricks were before him and he could now lead a spade towards his hand, promoting the 3 of trumps as a twelfth trick.

'King–queen to four is a good suit in your system?' queried Jacob Kessler.

'There are good good-suits and bad good-suits,' replied the Rabbi. 'David has perhaps learnt a slightly different version of Lebensohl from the one I know.'

The Rabbi played strongly on the second board of the round too, scoring an overtrick in 3NT.

'Two good boards already,' said David, as they were waiting for the next opponents to arrive. 'And yet my wife says that when it comes to bridge I have an inferiority complex.'

'Don't you believe it,' replied the Rabbi. 'No-one can make you feel inferior without your consent.'

The next visitors to the Rabbi's table were Miriam and the Cantor. Miriam blinked in disbelief at the sight of David sitting opposite the Rabbi. 'Eric is ill?' she said.

'Never healthier,' replied the Rabbi. 'I wanted to have a session with David, here. Sam kindly agreed to play with Eric.'

David beamed at Miriam. 'The Rabbi is checking my game,' he said. 'So far I have played all right, I think.'

'It is only the second round,' observed Miriam.

The players drew their cards for this deal:

Game all
Dealer West

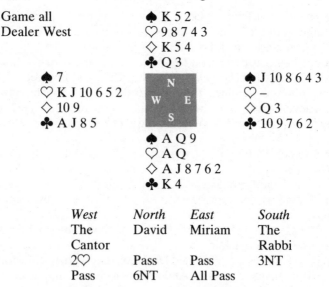

♠ K 5 2
♡ 9 8 7 4 3
◇ K 5 4
♣ Q 3

♠ 7
♡ K J 10 6 5 2
◇ 10 9
♣ A J 8 5

♠ J 10 8 6 4 3
♡ –
◇ Q 3
♣ 10 9 7 6 2

♠ A Q 9
♡ A Q
◇ A J 8 7 6 2
♣ K 4

West	North	East	South
The Cantor	David	Miriam	The Rabbi
2♡	Pass	Pass	3NT
Pass	6NT	All Pass	

The Cantor led ◇10 and David laid out his dummy. 'If you have nine tricks in your hand, Rabbi,' he said, 'my three high cards should bring the total to twelve.'

'Yes, thank you,' replied the Rabbi. There was nothing wrong with David's arithmetic. It was his judgement that was the problem.

The Rabbi won Miriam's queen of diamonds with the ace and quickly led a low club from his hand. The Cantor played low and dummy's queen won the trick.

Now I am batting, thought the Rabbi. He cashed the remainder of the diamond suit, followed by the three top spades. The Cantor, sitting West, was down to ♡K J ♣A J and had to find one more discard. His eventual choice was the jack of clubs. The Rabbi then threw him in with a club and scored two more tricks on the heart return.

Miriam's mouth fell open. 'Go in with the ace of clubs, Michael!' she exclaimed. 'Where is the end-play then?'

The Cantor raised his eyes to the ceiling. 'You mean somehow I should *know* he has six diamonds and two clubs?' he replied. 'How can I go in with the ace of clubs? It's almost certain to give away a trick.'

'That's how I would have defended, I can tell you,' said Miriam emphatically. 'In with the ace of clubs and you cannot be end-played.'

A few rounds later an ecstatic-looking Harry Grunfeld arrived at the table. 'Do you know who phoned me yesterday, Rabbi?' he asked, taking his seat. 'My daughter in Sydney. What good news she had for us.'

'Good news is to be shared,' said the Rabbi. 'There is too little of it around.'

'After four daughters she has at last produced a son!' said Grunfeld.

'Mazeltov, mazeltov,' declared the Rabbi. 'And tell me, how does the young man look? Like his grandfather?'

'I have no idea,' replied Grunfeld. 'No-one has looked at his face yet.'

Ernie Cole, Grunfeld's partner, bore the air of someone who had heard the news of the grandson one time too many. 'Shall we play?' he said.

North–South game
Dealer West

	♠ J 9 6 3	
	♡ K J 9 3	
	◇ Q 8	
	♣ 9 3 2	
♠ –		♠ Q 7 5 2
♡ 10 7 4 2	N	♡ 8 5
◇ A 10 7 5 3	W E	◇ 9 6 4 2
♣ A K J 4	S	♣ Q 6 5
	♠ A K 10 8 4	
	♡ A Q 6	
	◇ K J	
	♣ 10 8 7	

West	North	East	South
Ernie	David	Harry	The
Cole		Grunfeld	Rabbi
1◇	Pass	Pass	Dble
2♣	2♡	Pass	2♠
Pass	4♠	All Pass	

The Rabbi arrived in Four Spades and West led the ace of clubs. 'With any other partner I would not have bid so strongly,' declared David as he laid out his cards.

The Rabbi surveyed the 7-count with no great enthusiasm. Flattering as David's compliment was, he would willingly have swapped it for an extra high card in the dummy.

East played an encouraging 6 of clubs on the first trick and the Rabbi contributed the 7. The West player inspected these cards suspiciously. It would be just like the Rabbi to play the 7 from ♣Q 7 5, hoping to encourage a continuation. After contemplating the matter for a while, West switched to the ace and another diamond.

Breathing more freely, the Rabbi won the second diamond with the king. When the ace of trumps was cashed the news was less good, West showing out. The Rabbi crossed to dummy by over-taking the queen of hearts with the king. He then led the jack of trumps, followed by the 9, picking up the trump suit successfully. The Rabbi surveyed this end position:

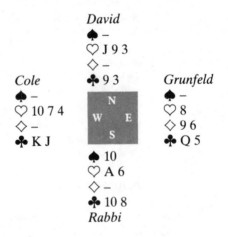

David
♠ –
♡ J 9 3
♢ –
♣ 9 3

Cole
♠ –
♡ 10 7 4
♢ –
♣ K J

Grunfeld
♠ –
♡ 8
♢ 9 6
♣ Q 5

Rabbi
♠ 10
♡ A 6
♢ –
♣ 10 8

When the Rabbi cashed the ace of hearts the 8 appeared from East. What to do on the next round? To finesse or not to finesse? The Rabbi cast his mind back to the early play. Suppose West had started with ♣A K J x x. Surely he would not have switched to diamonds. With three clubs visible in the dummy he would have known that a club continuation was safe. So, West's shape must be 0–4–5–4!

The Rabbi led his last heart and finessed dummy's 9. When East showed out, ten tricks were there.

'Four tricks off the top, I know,' said Ernie Cole. 'But your ♣6 was not clear. I had to guess.'

'What about my ♢2 on the next trick?' replied Harry Grunfeld. 'Was that unclear too?'

Cole nodded, realising his mistake. 'It reminds me of your new grandson,' he replied. 'I looked only at the club, not at the diamond.'

On the last round of the evening Sam and Eric arrived at the Rabbi's table. 'Such an enjoyable evening,' said Sam. 'I cannot remember such a session. One good score after another.'

David patted Sam on the shoulder. 'You have had such a bad run recently, Sam,' he observed. 'I am really pleased for you.'

Sam could not believe what he was hearing. A bad run, yes, but there was only one reason for that.

'From what you say, Sam,' continued David, 'your score must be almost as good as ours.'

On the first board of the round the Rabbi picked up:

♠ 7　　♡ A 10 7 3　　♢ 9 6 2　　♣ A K J 3 2

He opened One Club and Sam overcalled Two Clubs, a Michaels Cue-bid showing both the majors.

'Two Spades,' said David.

'What does this mean?' queried Eric.

'No idea, I'm afraid,' replied the Rabbi. 'David has learned some conventions for tonight's game. You may find something on our card, I don't know'.

Eric passed and the Rabbi marked time with a rebid of Three Clubs.

'Stop bid!' said David. 'Four Hearts.'

The Rabbi raised an eyebrow. Was this a splinter bid? David must have good club support anyway. Five Clubs was not the world's best contract at pairs. With three key cards in his hand there must be some play for the slam. 'Six Clubs,' said the Rabbi.

There was no further bidding. A trump was led and the other three players awaited the appearance of David's hand with interest.

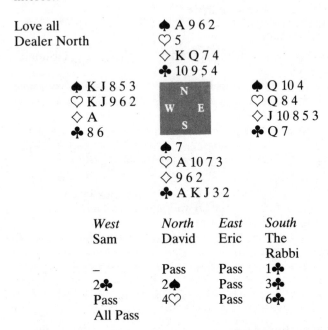

Love all
Dealer North

♠ A 9 6 2
♡ 5
◇ K Q 7 4
♣ 10 9 5 4

♠ K J 8 5 3
♡ K J 9 6 2
◇ A
♣ 8 6

♠ Q 10 4
♡ Q 8 4
◇ J 10 8 5 3
♣ Q 7

♠ 7
♡ A 10 7 3
◇ 9 6 2
♣ A K J 3 2

West	North	East	South
Sam	David	Eric	The Rabbi
–	Pass	Pass	1♣
2♣	2♠	Pass	3♣
Pass	4♡	Pass	6♣
All Pass			

Eric played the 7 on the trump lead, retaining the queen for a possible overruff on a fourth round of hearts. The Rabbi won the trick with the jack. 'What did your Two Spades mean, David?' he enquired.

David was crestfallen. 'You do not play that method, Rabbi?' he said. 'I read that Two Hearts shows a sound raise in clubs. Two Spades says that I also hold the diamonds.'

The Rabbi nodded politely, then turned his attention to the play. Since the very least he would need was to find West with the ace of diamonds, he led a diamond at trick 2. The ace duly appeared and Sam returned a second round of trumps. The contract still seemed hopeless. Diamonds could not break 3–3 and there were insufficient trumps to take all the ruffs that he needed.

Suddenly the Rabbi spotted a possibility. West was known to hold the length in both majors. Perhaps he could be put under pressure. The Rabbi cashed the king and queen of diamonds, West throwing one spade and one heart. These cards remained:

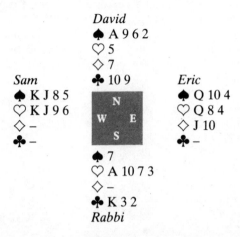

David
♠ A 9 6 2
♡ 5
♢ 7
♣ 10 9

Sam
♠ K J 8 5
♡ K J 9 6
♢ –
♣ –

Eric
♠ Q 10 4
♡ Q 8 4
♢ J 10
♣ –

♠ 7
♡ A 10 7 3
♢ –
♣ K 3 2
Rabbi

Since neither major could be ruffed good at this stage, the Rabbi tried something different. He ruffed the last diamond! Sam did not like the look of this. If he threw a spade, declarer would be able to set up the spade suit with two ruffs. And it seemed that a similar fate would await him if he discarded a heart.

With a sinking feeling Sam threw a heart. The Rabbi now cashed the ace of hearts and proceeded to set up a long card in hearts, using spade ruffs as entries. As if by magic, he had transformed eleven tricks into twelve.

'I knew you would make it!' exclaimed David. 'My Four Hearts was a splinter bid. You would have made the same call, surely.'

The Rabbi laughed. 'Much as I appreciate when a 9-count is a good 9-count,' he replied, 'I'm not sure I would have made a slam try on your hand.'

It was a moment to remember for a long time, thought David. He had made a better bid than the Rabbi would have done! 'At least there was no problem in the play,' he said.

On the final hand of the evening, vulnerable against not, the Rabbi picked up these cards:

♠ K Q 8 7 6 3   ♡ 2   ♢ A J 10 4   ♣ A 6

He opened One Spade and Sam, to his left, made an intermediate overcall of Three Hearts. David passed and Eric raised to Four Hearts. The Rabbi surveyed his cards once more. On an unlucky day Four Spades doubled could cost 800. Still, if David held just three small spades and ◇K the game might even make. No doubt he should pass, but . . . 'Four Spades,' said the Rabbi.

No-one saw fit to double, the Rabbi was pleased to see, and this was the full deal:

North–South game   ♠ A 10 9 5 2
Dealer East   ♡ 8 5
                     ◇ 7 6 2
                     ♣ J 8 4

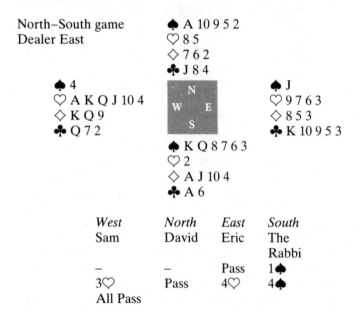

♠ 4   ♠ J
♡ A K Q J 10 4   ♡ 9 7 6 3
◇ K Q 9   ◇ 8 5 3
♣ Q 7 2   ♣ K 10 9 5 3

                        ♠ K Q 8 7 6 3
                        ♡ 2
                        ◇ A J 10 4
                        ♣ A 6

West	North	East	South
Sam	David	Eric	The Rabbi
–	–	Pass	1♠
3♡	Pass	4♡	4♠
All Pass			

Sam led the ace of hearts and down went the dummy.

'No need for you to bid Four Spades, Rabbi, I would have bid it myself,' declared David. 'Don't you trust my bidding?'

The Rabbi gazed in disbelief at the 5-card support in the dummy. 'You did not think of raising on the previous round?' he enquired.

'A double raise on just 5 points?' exclaimed David. 'You think I am a beginner or something?'

At trick 2 Sam continued with the king of hearts. After a few moments consideration the Rabbi discarded ♣6 on this trick. When Sam switched to a trump the Rabbi won in the South hand. He then cashed the ace of clubs and crossed to dummy twice in trumps to eliminate the club suit. With hearts and clubs removed from the scene, the Rabbi crossed to dummy with a fourth round of trumps. He then led a diamond to the jack. Sam won with the queen and the Rabbi now faced his remaining cards, claiming the balance. Sam had two losing choices. He could play a diamond into the tenace or concede a ruff-and-discard.

'A club switch at trick 2 beats it, I know,' declared an annoyed Sam. 'You would switch to a club from my hand, Rabbi?'

'Very dangerous from queen-to-three,' replied the Rabbi. 'Even so, I think I might have found a way to beat it.'

'There was another way?' queried Sam.

'Playing with Eric, I would lead the king of hearts, asking for count,' replied the Rabbi. 'When I see the 7 I know he must hold four hearts. So, a low heart at trick 2.'

'Now declarer cannot duck,' said Eric. 'If he lets my 9 win I will switch to diamonds.'

Sam was happy to receive instruction from the Rabbi. He was distinctly less keen to have Eric lecturing him. 'I play the same method myself,' he declared. 'I didn't think Eric would know it.'

David's face dropped as he inspected the score-sheet. 'It is not a top, Rabbi,' he reported. 'One pair has made Four Spades doubled.'

'Life is full of disappointments,' observed the Rabbi. 'We must all make the best of what we are given.'

'Quite so, Rabbi,' said Sam. 'And tonight you have set us an excellent example!'

8.   The Unimportant Match

'Ah, Rabbi, I have a small matter to discuss with you,' said Eric. 'Have you ever played against Lionel Berg?'

'Many times,' chuckled the Rabbi. 'It is hard to believe someone so intelligent can play bridge so badly. His motto should be: why win a trick when you can lose it.'

'I see you have played against him,' said Eric. 'Anyway, he has friends at the Central Synagogue in Hendon. He wants to arrange a match between us and them.'

'And he would want to be in our team, I suppose,' replied the Rabbi. 'What chance would we have then? The Central Synagogue has some strong players.'

'Maybe we could restrict the teams in some way,' suggested Eric. 'We could say it must be one men's pair, one ladies' pair, one mixed pair, and . . .'

The Rabbi smiled. 'And one idiot pair?' he said.

'We could put it more diplomatically,' replied Eric. 'Perhaps er . . . one pair that does not play duplicate.'

The match was duly arranged and took place some two weeks later. On the first round Eric and the Rabbi faced the strong partnership of Edwin Roth and David Lehrmann.

'Edwin, my friend,' exclaimed the Rabbi. 'I was not expecting to see you. I thought that Martin and Simon would be your men's pair.'

'They are playing too,' replied Roth. 'David and I are the non-duplicate pair.'

The Rabbi's mouth dropped. 'But you are both Lifemasters,' he said. 'You play duplicate every week.'

'If only,' replied Roth, shaking his head. 'With business so hectic, I haven't played duplicate for ages.'

'Nor me,' added Lehrmann. 'Such bad flu I caught recently. I have not been to the club for almost two weeks.'

The Rabbi inspected his cards for the first board:

♠ Q 9 2   ♡ K 9 5   ♢ A K 3   ♣ A Q J 8

'One Heart,' said Eric.

The Rabbi responded with a Baron 2NT, showing a balanced hand of 16 points or more.

'Three no-trumps,' said Eric.

So, thought the Rabbi, he has a minimum. Still, was the man not allowed to have a good heart suit? With 19 points no-one could accuse him of overbidding if he made one more try with 4NT. 'Six no-trumps,' said the Rabbi.

The Rabbi blinked. Had he said Six? He had meant to say Four. Ah, well.

Lehrmann led ♠5 and this was the full deal:

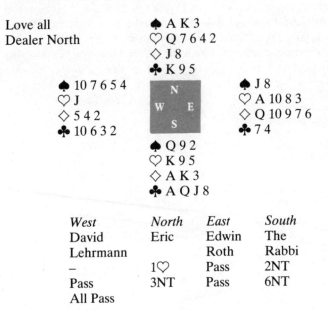

Love all
Dealer North

♠ A K 3
♡ Q 7 6 4 2
♢ J 8
♣ K 9 5

♠ 10 7 6 5 4   ♠ J 8
♡ J   ♡ A 10 8 3
♢ 5 4 2   ♢ Q 10 9 7 6
♣ 10 6 3 2   ♣ 7 4

♠ Q 9 2
♡ K 9 5
♢ A K 3
♣ A Q J 8

West	North	East	South
David	Eric	Edwin	The
Lehrmann		Roth	Rabbi
–	1♡	Pass	2NT
Pass	3NT	Pass	6NT
All Pass			

The Rabbi was disappointed to find such moderate hearts in the dummy. It seemed that the only chance was to find a defender with ace doubleton of hearts. By leading the first round through the ace, he would be able to score four tricks in the suit.

The Rabbi won the first trick with the spade queen and led a heart towards dummy. The jack appeared from West and dummy's queen was taken by the ace. Putting declarer to an immediate guess, Roth returned ♡3. The key point of the hand had been reached. Restricted Choice made a singleton jack of hearts twice as likely as West having chosen to play the jack from jack–10 doubleton. Against that, if the Rabbi rose with the king and did drop the 10 from West he would have twelve tricks on top. This would not be the case after a successful finesse of the 9.

Still, thought the Rabbi, there was something about the way in which Roth had so quickly returned a heart. If he did indeed hold ♡A83 Roth would surely have switched elsewhere, expecting that if partner did hold the 10 he would score it in due course. Or, yes, he might even have held off the ace, creating the impression that West held A J doubleton.

Following his judgement, the Rabbi finessed ♡9. This won the trick and West discarded ♣4. When the Rabbi continued with the king of hearts, West retained his length in both the black suits, throwing a small diamond. The Rabbi cashed four rounds of clubs, then crossed to dummy with the ace of spades. This was the end position:

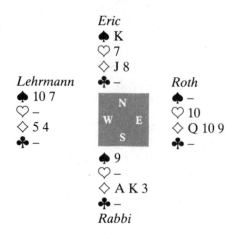

Eric
♠ K
♡ 7
♢ J 8
♣ –

Lehrmann
♠ 10 7
♡ –
♢ 5 4
♣ –

Roth
♠ –
♡ 10
♢ Q 10 9
♣ –

♠ 9
♡ –
♢ A K 3
♣ –
Rabbi

The king of spades left Roth with no good discard. He threw a diamond, retaining a guard on the threat that he could actually see, but the Rabbi was then able to cash three diamond tricks.

Roth glared at his partner. 'How can you do this?' he demanded. 'You throw your diamond guard and I am squeezed.'

'Diamond guard?' replied Lehrmann. 'I had three small.'

'It was a guard, believe me,' persisted Roth. 'Didn't you see? He made ◇3 at the end.'

The Rabbi chuckled to himself. 'You ask too much, Edwin,' he retorted. 'How can you expect a non-duplicate player to realise he must keep three diamonds to the five?'

In such a match it was essential for the tigers to extract large numbers of IMPs from the rabbits. The Central Synagogue's top pair, Simon Jacobson and Martin Reimann, had already taken a couple of good boards against Lionel Berg and his partner. Jacobson was hoping for more of the same as he bid a slam on this hand:

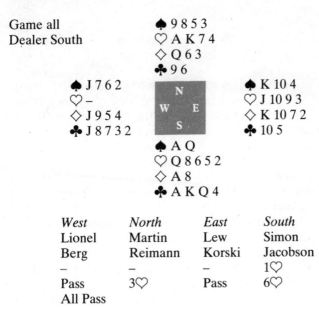

Game all
Dealer South

North
♠ 9 8 5 3
♡ A K 7 4
◇ Q 6 3
♣ 9 6

West
♠ J 7 6 2
♡ —
◇ J 9 5 4
♣ J 8 7 3 2

East
♠ K 10 4
♡ J 10 9 3
◇ K 10 7 2
♣ 10 5

South
♠ A Q
♡ Q 8 6 5 2
◇ A 8
♣ A K Q 4

West	North	East	South
Lionel	Martin	Lew	Simon
Berg	Reimann	Korski	Jacobson
–	–	–	1♡
Pass	3♡	Pass	6♡
All Pass			

A spade was led, East's king drawing declarer's ace. Jacobson played a trump to the ace, raising an eyebrow when West showed out. What could be done? Perhaps he could end-play East with a trump to lead away from the king of diamonds.

Jacobson cashed the queen of spades, returned to dummy with the trump king, and ruffed a spade. He then drew a third round of trumps with the queen and started on the clubs. This was the position with one high club still to be played:

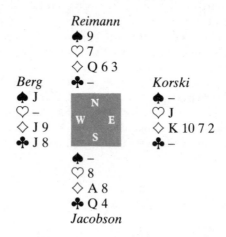

Reimann
♠ 9
♡ 7
◇ Q 6 3
♣ —

Berg
♠ J
♡ —
◇ J 9
♣ J 8

Korski
♠ —
♡ J
◇ K 10 7 2
♣ —

Jacobson
♠ —
♡ 8
◇ A 8
♣ Q 4

When the queen of clubs was led, East could not gain by ruffing. He would have to lead away from the king of diamonds and declarer would then make his last two trumps separately. Korski decided to throw a diamond on the club queen. Now came the last club, ruffed with dummy's 9 of trumps. Again East had no counter. If he failed to overruff, declarer would score his last trump *en passant* by leading a spade. East did in fact overruff but the diamond exit was run successfully to the queen and declarer had twelve tricks.

'I didn't think much of that spade lead,' observed Lew Korski. 'You trapped my king.'

'He would guess it right anyway,' declared Lionel Berg. 'They say that only weak players lead from a jack, but what could I do? Jacks in all three suits, I had.'

Jacobson looked disdainfully at his opponent. 'Diamond lead cracks it,' he observed.

'A diamond lead makes it easy for you,' declared Lew Korski. 'You win my king with the ace and dummy's queen is good.'

Was the guy trying to be funny, thought Jacobson. Apparently not. 'You play the 10, not the king,' he replied. 'The 10 forces my ace.'

Lew Korski studied the four curtain cards. 'Yes, that would be clever,' he said eventually. 'I made the same mistake in spades, now I think of it. I played the king rather than the 10.'

The battle was at its most intense when the two ladies pairs met on the second round. Not that a casual onlooker would have guessed it from the universal smiles on display.

'Such a pleasant atmosphere in this match,' declared Judith. 'No-one cares about the result. That is why.'

'Did I not make just the same point to you, Libbie?' observed Suzie Lutz. 'It is how bridge is meant to be.'

With the frozen smiles still in place, the four ladies reached for their cards.

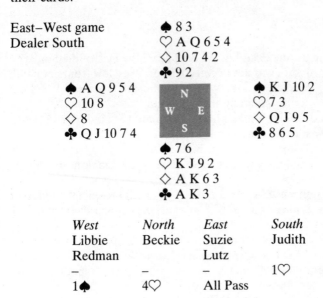

East–West game
Dealer South

```
                  ♠ 8 3
                  ♡ A Q 6 5 4
                  ◇ 10 7 4 2
                  ♣ 9 2
  ♠ A Q 9 5 4                    ♠ K J 10 2
  ♡ 10 8          N             ♡ 7 3
  ◇ 8          W     E          ◇ Q J 9 5
  ♣ Q J 10 7 4    S             ♣ 8 6 5
                  ♠ 7 6
                  ♡ K J 9 2
                  ◇ A K 6 3
                  ♣ A K 3
```

West	North	East	South
Libbie	Beckie	Suzie	Judith
Redman		Lutz	
–	–	–	1♡
1♠	4♡	All Pass	

Judith won the club lead with the ace and drew trumps in two rounds. If diamonds were 3–2, life would be easy. What to do if they were 4–1?

Judith cashed the other top club and ruffed a club. She then played a diamond to the ace, the 8 falling from West. The time had come to exit with a spade. East won two spade tricks with the 10 and the jack. These cards were still out:

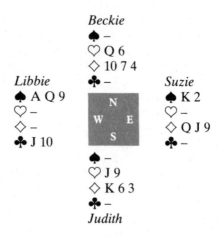

Beckie
♠ —
♡ Q 6
♢ 10 7 4
♣ —

Libbie
♠ A Q 9
♡ —
♢ —
♣ J 10

Suzie
♠ K 2
♡ —
♢ Q J 9
♣ —

♠ —
♡ J 9
♢ K 6 3
♣ —
Judith

Hoping for the best, Suzie Lutz placed the jack of diamonds on the table. Judith was not deceived. She played low from her hand, allowing the jack to win. When West showed out she faced her remaining cards, claiming the contract.

'What a lead you make here!' exclaimed Suzie Lutz. 'Ace and king of spades we play and she cannot do it.'

Libbie Redman shook her head. 'Still it is easy,' she declared. 'After eliminating the clubs she plays a low diamond to the 10. You are end-played.'

'Such nonsense,' replied Lutz. 'I win with the queen and return the 5. She is putting in the 6? She wants to go down when diamonds are 3–2?'

Judith sat back contentedly enjoying every word of the opponents' heated *post mortem*. 'Not to worry,' she said, when they eventually fell silent. 'At least it did not happen in some match where the result mattered.'

The Rabbi and Eric faced the opposing mixed pair in their second match.

'Which pair are you?' enquired the enormous George Mosimann. 'The experts or the non-experts?'

'What a question to ask!' exclaimed his wife, Trudi. 'Let me apologise for him, gentlemen.'

'No offence taken,' replied the Rabbi.

This was the first board of the round:

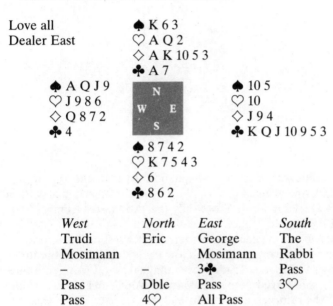

Love all
Dealer East

♠ K 6 3
♡ A Q 2
◇ A K 10 5 3
♣ A 7

♠ A Q J 9
♡ J 9 8 6
◇ Q 8 7 2
♣ 4

♠ 10 5
♡ 10
◇ J 9 4
♣ K Q J 10 9 5 3

♠ 8 7 4 2
♡ K 7 5 4 3
◇ 6
♣ 8 6 2

West	North	East	South
Trudi	*Eric*	*George*	*The*
Mosimann		Mosimann	Rabbi
–	–	3♣	Pass
Pass	Dble	Pass	3♡
Pass	4♡	All Pass	

The Rabbi arrived in Four Hearts and won the club lead in the dummy. He cashed the ace and king of diamonds and ruffed a diamond, both defenders following all the while. A trump to the ace dropped the 10 from East. If East is 1–2–3–7, thought the Rabbi, he could draw trumps with the king and queen, ruff the diamonds good and re-enter dummy with the spade king. Still, that trump 10 smells like a singleton. Let's play East for 2–1–3–7 shape.

The Rabbi ruffed another diamond and led a spade towards dummy's king. West went in with the ace and exited with the queen of spades to dummy's king. This was the end position:

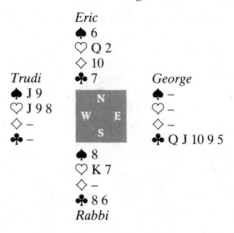

It would not be good enough now to lead the established diamond, throwing a spade. West would ruff and exit with a trump. Declarer would score only the two master trumps. 'Play the club,' said the Rabbi.

East had to win and return another club. West ruffed, to prevent declarer from scoring dummy's low trump, and the Rabbi threw dummy's last spade. Trudi Mosimann had no effective continuation. If she played a spade, declarer would make three trump tricks. She returned a trump instead, but now the Rabbi was able to draw trumps and enjoy the established diamond.

'Yes, ten tricks,' said Trudi Mosimann. 'You have guessed which pair they are yet, George?'

The Rabbi and Eric had performed heroically but at half time they found that their side was 11 IMPs adrift.

'Disappointing, Rabbi,' observed Lionel Berg. 'Lew and I did not have a good card, I realise, but we are the non-expert pair.'

Lew Korski nodded. 'Yes,' he said. 'We were hoping you and Eric might rescue us.'

The Rabbi maintained an impassive expression. Was it possible to rescue from drowning someone who had a one-ton weight on each leg? 'Perhaps in the second half we can all do better,' he said.

9. Lionel Berg's Good Second Half

Hoping for better luck to come his way in the second half, Lionel Berg resumed his seat. His opponents were the Central Synagogue's mixed pair, Trudi and George Mosimann.

Love all
Dealer North

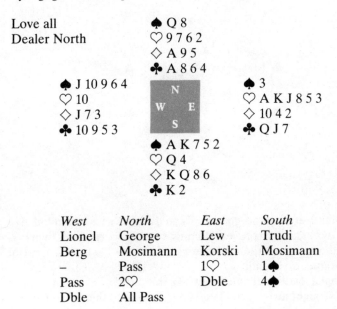

```
              ♠ Q 8
              ♡ 9 7 6 2
              ◇ A 9 5
              ♣ A 8 6 4
♠ J 10 9 6 4                    ♠ 3
♡ 10              N             ♡ A K J 8 5 3
◇ J 7 3        W   E            ◇ 10 4 2
♣ 10 9 5 3        S             ♣ Q J 7
              ♠ A K 7 5 2
              ♡ Q 4
              ◇ K Q 8 6
              ♣ K 2
```

West	North	East	South
Lionel	George	Lew	Trudi
Berg	Mosimann	Korski	Mosimann
–	Pass	1♡	1♠
Pass	2♡	Dble	4♠
Dble	All Pass		

George Mosimann had an awkward call to make on the second round. Although he had only 2-card spade support he could think of no better bid than a fit-showing cue bid. His wife needed no further encouragement to bid the game and was somewhat surprised when Lionel Berg doubled.

Berg led the jack of trumps, won with dummy's queen. Trudi Mosimann surveyed the dummy through her gold-rimmed spectacles. West doubtless held five trumps, but maybe the side suits would break favourably. When she cashed three rounds of diamonds both defenders followed all the way. She then played the king and ace of clubs, followed by a club ruff in hand. Her next move was to exit with the queen of hearts. East won with the king and cashed a second round of hearts. When he continued with a third round, Trudi Mosimann ruffed with the ace. These cards remained:

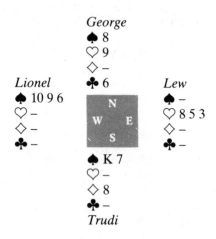

George
♠ 8
♡ 9
♢ –
♣ 6

Lionel
♠ 10 9 6
♡ –
♢ –
♣ –

Lew
♠ –
♡ 8 5 3
♢ –
♣ –

♠ K 7
♡ –
♢ 8
♣ –
Trudi

Lionel Berg had no good reply to declarer's last diamond. He ruffed with the 9, to prevent dummy's 8 from scoring, but then had to lead away from the 10 of trumps. It was +590 for the Central Synagogue mixed pair.

'What a lead!' exclaimed Lew Korski. 'Lead a heart and it is one down straight away. I bid hearts and I doubled their Two Hearts. What more can I do to ask for a heart lead?'

'But I wanted to cut down the ruffs,' replied Berg.

Lew Korski turned towards the North player, seeking support. 'I bid hearts *and* I doubled hearts,' he said. 'You would not lead a heart from his hand?'

George Mosimann shrugged his enormous shoulders. 'Certainly I would give some thought to it,' he said.

Meanwhile the Rabbi and Eric faced the opposing ladies pair.

'You must treat us gently, Rabbi,' said the elegantly attired Libbie Redman. 'None of your clever plays against two ladies, please.'

This was the first hand they played:

East–West game   ♠ K 9 6 4
Dealer South   ♡ 8
                          ◇ A K 8
                          ♣ Q J 6 4 3

♠ 10 5		♠ A J 7 3
♡ A J 9 7 6 4	N	♡ 10 5
◇ 9 5	W E	◇ 10 6 2
♣ 8 7 5	S	♣ A 10 9 2

                    ♠ Q 8 2
                    ♡ K Q 3 2
                    ◇ Q J 7 4 3
                    ♣ K

West	*North*	*East*	*South*
Libbie	Eric	Suzie	The
Redman		Lutz	Rabbi
–	–	–	1◇
Pass	2♣	Pass	2◇
Pass	2♠	Pass	2NT
Pass	3NT	All Pass	

Libbie Redman led ♡7 against 3NT, her partner's 10 drawing
the Rabbi's king. At trick 2 the king of clubs was allowed to hold.
What next, thought the Rabbi.

It seemed from the opening lead that West held five or six hearts
to the A J. If she held only five hearts the defence was certain to
prevail, so give her six hearts. With another ace in her hand she
would surely have overcalled, so place the two black aces with
East.

The Rabbi was now planning on double-dummy lines. What if
he crossed to a diamond and played the club queen to East's ace?
All would be well if she played back a heart; West would not be
able to cash a second heart without setting up South's ♡Q for a
ninth trick. Perhaps East would return a club, though. The
defenders would then have five tricks to take when they regained
the lead.

The Rabbi gave a small sigh. It would be the same if he played
on spades. Even after a diamond to the ace and a spade to the
queen, the defenders would be poised to score two hearts, two
spades and a club.

Suddenly an amazing thought came to the Rabbi. Since he would be safe if East were to play a heart through, why not play a heart himself? At trick 3 the Rabbi made an unusual play – he led ♡2 from his hand! West won with the 6 but, as the Rabbi had foreseen, she was now cut off from her partner. If she were to cash the ace of hearts she would give declarer an eighth trick, with an easy ninth to come in one of the black suits.

Libbie Redman chose instead to exit passively with a diamond. The Rabbi won with dummy's ace and led the queen of clubs. East won with the ace and cleared a second club trick for herself, but the Rabbi now played on spades, bringing his own total to nine.

Libbie Redman spread her hands. 'What was this heart play, Rabbi?' she asked. 'Had hearts been 5–3 we would have run the suit.'

'True,' replied the Rabbi. 'But if hearts were 5–3 the contract could not be made.'

'I thought we agreed no clever plays,' persisted Libbie Redman. 'What chance do we have against that?'

'Jacobson or Reimann will find the same move,' replied the Rabbi. 'Even your non-duplicate pair, maybe, if they are sitting North–South.'

Suzie Lutz looked a bit sheepish. 'I was not too happy to see them as our non-experts,' she said.

Libbie Redman nodded her agreement. 'Particularly as you chose a pair so accurately fitting that description,' she added.

The fourth and final round of the match saw the two mixed pairs meet. The players extracted their cards for this deal:

North–South game   ♠ J 6 5 4
Dealer South   ♡ A K 7 5 3 2
                        ◇ 10 6 4
                        ♣ –

West		East
♠ 10		♠ K 8
♡ Q J 10 9 4		♡ 8 6
◇ A 9 8 5		◇ K Q J 7 2
♣ K 9 4		♣ A J 6 2

                   ♠ A Q 9 7 3 2
                   ♡ –
                   ◇ 3
                   ♣ Q 10 8 7 5 3

West	North	East	South
Trudi	Miriam	George	The
Mosimann		Mosimann	Cantor
–	–	–	1♠
2♡	4♣	4◇	4♠
5◇	5♠	Pass	6♠
Pass	Pass	Dble	All Pass

Miriam's Four Clubs was a splinter bid, agreeing spades as trumps and showing at most one club. The Cantor restrained himself at first, bidding only Four Spades at his second turn. When Miriam went to the Five level he was not to be held back. Did he not have a four-loser hand? He bid Six Spades and George Mosimann doubled in the pass-out seat.

The elegantly-groomed Trudi Mosimann led the ace of diamonds, pleased to see this card stand up. There was still the whole of her husband's double to come; the penalty should be substantial. Or – wait a minute – perhaps the double had been Lightner. Perhaps George had a void heart.

At trick two Mrs Mosimann switched to the queen of hearts. Trying to ignore Miriam's eyes on him, the Cantor won with dummy's ace, throwing a club. He then cashed the king of hearts successfully, throwing another club. Why did Miriam always watch him with such a worried expression? He played the cards as well as she did. Well, most of the time, anyway.

The Cantor cross-ruffed three hearts and three clubs. East could not afford to discard any clubs while the hearts were being ruffed.

If he did, declarer's club suit would become established; he would then simply revert to drawing trumps. At trick 10 the lead was in dummy and these cards remained:

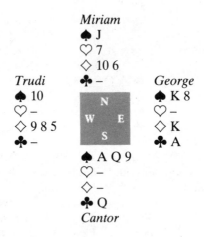

Miriam
♠ J
♡ 7
♢ 10 6
♣ —

Trudi
♠ 10
♡ —
♢ 9 8 5
♣ —

George
♠ K 8
♡ —
♢ K
♣ A

♠ A Q 9
♡ —
♢ —
♣ Q
Cantor

The Cantor ruffed a diamond with the 9, ruffed his last club in dummy, and called for a diamond. East's king was trapped under declarer's ace–queen and twelve tricks resulted.

'Such a nice play, Michael!' exclaimed a delighted Miriam. 'I knew you would make it.'

The enormous George Mosimann was less amused. 'What was this heart at trick 2, Trudi?' he complained. 'Play a trump and he can only ruff three clubs.'

'Five hearts I had, and six in the dummy,' replied his wife. 'After your Lightner Double I put you with a void, of course.'

'What are you saying, Lightner Double?' exclaimed Mosimann. 'You overcall vulnerable and I have 14 points? Am I not allowed to double a slam?'

At the same time the two 'novice' pairs faced each other. Lionel Berg's partners rarely carried him to the slam level, for the good reason that he scarcely ever made twelve tricks. Lew Korski thought he had spotted an exception to the rule on this deal:

East–West game
Dealer South

♠ K 8 5
♡ 9
♢ A K Q 10 7 2
♣ A 9 3

♠ Q J 2   ♠ 10 4
♡ K 8 6 3   N   ♡ J 10 4
♢ 9 3   W   E   ♢ J 8 6 5
♣ K Q 10 6   S   ♣ 8 7 5 2

♠ A 9 7 6 3
♡ A Q 7 5 2
♢ 4
♣ J 4

West	North	East	South
David	Lew	Edwin	Lionel
Lehrmann	Korski	Roth	Berg
–	–	–	1♠
Pass	3♢	Pass	3♡
Pass	4NT	Pass	5♡
Pass	5NT	Pass	6♣
Pass	6♠	All Pass	

Lehrmann led the king of clubs against Six Spades and Lionel Berg won with dummy's ace. Both defenders followed to the ace and king of trumps, he was pleased to see, and he now turned to the diamond suit. The ace and king stood up and he discarded his losing club. What to do next? If diamonds were 3–3 he would be able to throw his four heart losers, the defenders scoring just a trump trick. But what if diamonds were 4–2? Perhaps he should ruff the third round of the suit and return to dummy with a heart ruff. No, that was no good. The defenders would interrupt the flow of the diamonds with the last trump; there would then be no entry back to dummy. 'Queen of diamonds, please,' said Berg.

Edwin Roth ruffed the diamond queen with his master trump and exited with the queen of clubs. Berg ruffed in the South hand and could then ruff one heart. Two heart losers remained, unfortunately, and the slam was two down.

Roth looked across at this partner. 'If he ruffs a low diamond instead of trying to cash the queen, you don't overruff, right?'

'Of course not,' replied Lehrmann. 'What kind of *patzer* you think I am?'

Berg was reassured by this exchange. 'Ah, so I couldn't make it, then?' he said.

'No, you couldn't make it,' replied Roth.

Lehrmann leaned forward. 'Ace of clubs, ace of diamonds, ruff a diamond, ace–king of trumps, run the diamonds,' he said. What's wrong with that?'

Roth looked irritated. 'I didn't say it couldn't be made,' he replied. 'I said he couldn't make it.'

Not far away the two men's pairs faced each other.

'Oy vey, that Berg is bad player,' said Simon Jacobson. 'I thought he would be when I saw him. Such a small head he has.'

The Rabbi directed a look of reprimand at his opponent. 'You cannot judge people by their physical characteristics,' he declared. 'Except perhaps that you can tell an ass by his long ears and a fool by his big tongue.'

'True enough, Rabbi,' replied Jacobson. 'You to speak.'

North–South game
Dealer South

♠ K 10 8 7
♡ Q J 8
♢ A 7 6 4 2
♣ J

♠ 5 3
♡ 9 7 6 4
♢ 10
♣ Q 10 9 7 4 3

♠ Q 9 2
♡ A K 10 2
♢ Q J 9 8
♣ K 8

♠ A J 6 4
♡ 5 3
♢ K 5 3
♣ A 6 5 2

West	North	East	South
Simon	Eric	Martin	The
Jacobson		Reimann	Rabbi
–	–	–	1♣
Pass	1♢	1NT	Pass
Pass	Dble	Pass	Pass
2♣	Pass	Pass	2♠
Pass	4♠	All Pass	

Jacobson led $\diamond$10, a card that looked suspiciously like a singleton, and the Rabbi won with the king. East's 1NT bid suggested he would hold the trump queen. The Rabbi crossed to the king of trumps, finessed the jack of trumps successfully, and drew East's last trump with the ace. He continued with a diamond, ducking in the dummy. Reimann won and returned the king of clubs to declarer's ace. Ace of diamonds and a diamond ruff, followed by a club ruff, and cashing the $\diamond$7, reduced dummy to $\heartsuit$Q J 8 and East to $\heartsuit$A K 10. The Rabbi called for the queen of hearts and Reimann had to concede defeat. Ten tricks had been made.

'Yes,' sighed Martin Reimann. 'I helped you too much with that 1NT bid.'

Jacobson gave a rueful nod. 'At least you do not have big ears, Martin,' he said.

'Well, we have done much better in the second half,' announced Lionel Berg, as he and his partner returned for the final scoring. 'We let two games through against the Mosimanns, but apart from that not too bad.'

'Except for the Three Hearts doubled that Roth made,' Korski reminded him. 'That might not be flat. Nor the spade slam you went down in.'

A detailed examination of the Berg score-card failed to reveal any improvement from the first half. A few moments later Simon Jacobson strolled over. 'Very close and enjoyable match, Rabbi,' he said. 'We win by 5, do you make it?'

The Rabbi nodded. 'Your team played well,' he replied. 'Particularly your non-expert pair.'

Jacobson gave a half-embarrassed smile. 'We had Bessie Zuckerberg and her partner as our non-experts,' he said. 'At the last minute she could not make it. She had to visit her Mother.'

'It was fortunate you had such adequate replacements available,' observed the Rabbi.

'Come, it was fun anyway,' declared Jacobson. 'Promise me you will play the same match next year. Bessie Zuckerberg is on our team sheet, I guarantee it.'

Smiling, the Rabbi rose to his feet and shook Jacobson's hand. 'Of course,' he replied. 'You should see our ladies pair next year, Simon. What Meckstroth and Rodwell will look like in short skirts, I can hardly imagine!'

10.   View of the Mediterranean

Every two or three years the Rabbi took a prolonged holiday to Israel, visiting his many friends there. On the present occasion he was staying with Joe and Katya Simmonds. Joe had been a successful lawyer back in England but had retired many years ago. The couple now lived in Natanya, in a simple flat that overlooked the Mediterranean.

The Rabbi admired the view, the sea sparkling in the afternoon sunshine. 'What a sight!' he exclaimed. 'Perhaps, one day, I could retire and follow you here.'

Joe Simmonds smiled. 'You could be among friends if you did, Rabbi,' he replied. 'Many of them are looking forward to seeing you tonight at the Club.'

The Rabbi's eyes lit up. 'I remember last time I played there,' he replied. 'That amazing old man . . . I forget his name, he made Six Clubs against us. Does he still play?'

'No, no, he died a while back,' replied Simmonds. 'Must have been shortly after you last came.'

'Well, he could die happy after that Six Clubs,' declared the Rabbi. 'I could not believe it. At the time I was annoyed I had not found the diamond lead but, well, I cannot begrudge the old man his triumph now.'

That evening the Natanya Bridge Club was crowded, many occasional players having turned up to meet the Rabbi from England. The first round brought Sol and Edie Klein to the Rabbi's table. The Rabbi was pleased to find that the change of country had not affected his ability to pick up good hands. This was the first board:

Love all
Dealer East

```
                    ♠ 8 4
                    ♡ 9 3
                    ◇ 9 7 6 4 3
                    ♣ A 10 9 7
♠ Q 9 7 3                              ♠ J 5
♡ Q 10 8 6 4 2      N                  ♡ A J 5
◇ 5 2            W     E               ◇ K J 10 8
♣ 4                 S                  ♣ Q 6 5 3
                    ♠ A K 10 6 2
                    ♡ K 7
                    ◇ A Q
                    ♣ K J 8 2
```

West	North	East	South
Sol	Joe	Edie	The
Klein	Simmonds	Klein	Rabbi
–	–	1◇	Dble
1♡	Pass	2♡	2NT
Pass	3NT	All Pass	

Sol Klein led ♡6 and stared at the dummy with a puzzled expression. 'You give him three on that?' he queried.

Joe Simmonds nodded confidently. 'Perhaps you have not seen the Rabbi play before,' he replied. 'He does not need points like most people do.'

East won the heart lead with the ace and returned the jack of hearts to the Rabbi's king. How to play it? East would have to hold the king of diamonds and was surely a strong favourite for the club queen too. The only problem would be if East held four clubs to the queen rather than two or three. How could he arrange three minor-suit leads from the table?

The Rabbi soon spotted the answer. At trick 3 he led the jack of clubs and overtook with dummy's ace. He then led the 10 of clubs. When East followed with a small card the Rabbi unblocked the 8 from the South hand. West showed out but the Rabbi was now in command of the hand. He led the 9 of clubs, covered by the queen and king, and could then return to the club 7 to take the diamond finesse. This succeeded and he now had nine tricks.

'You see what I mean?' said Joe Simmonds happily.

'It was not so clever,' declared Sol Klein. 'He leads the jack of clubs to see if I cover, then finesses the other way when I don't. Everyone knows to do that.'

'You are from England?' enquired Edie Klein, a small woman dressed in very bright clothes.

'That's right,' replied the Rabbi.

'Ah, England!' exclaimed Edie Klein. 'You don't by any chance know Hymie Glick, do you?'

'I'm afraid not,' replied the Rabbi.

'A big man,' continued Edie Klein. 'Not much hair and always wears a blue suit. He is a cousin of mine. Very good company, you would like him.'

The Rabbi smiled politely at the elderly lady. 'I will look out for him when I return,' he said.

Joe's propensity for overbidding brought mixed results on the next few rounds. The Rabbi estimated their score at slightly below average when the owner of the club arrived at their table.

'Ah, Freddie,' said Joe Simmonds. 'You remember the Rabbi here, from England?'

'How can I forget?' declared Freddie Buchner. 'You recall the last time you were here? We played rubber bridge until the sun rose?'

'Of course,' replied the Rabbi. 'I slept the whole way back on the plane.'

'You remember that Four Spades?' continued Buchner. 'You went off. I told you how you could make it.'

'Well, I never did agree with you on that,' replied the Rabbi, laughing. 'Anyway, let's play.'

North–South game
Dealer South

```
                    ♠ K 9 8 6
                    ♡ 9 7 2
                    ◇ 8
                    ♣ Q J 7 6 5
    ♠ 10 7 4                        ♠ J 2
    ♡ K J 6          N              ♡ 10 8 4
    ◇ Q J 10 3     W   E            ◇ K 9 6 5 4
    ♣ A 9 2          S              ♣ K 10 4
                    ♠ A Q 5 3
                    ♡ A Q 5 3
                    ◇ A 7 2
                    ♣ 8 3
```

West	North	East	South
Freddie	Joe	Amnon	The
Buchner	Simmonds	Lerner	Rabbi
–	–	–	1NT
Pass	2♣	Pass	2♠
Pass	4♠	All Pass	

Buchner led the queen of diamonds and looked with amusement at the 6-count in the dummy. 'You are playing the English weak no-trump, Joe?' he quipped.

'You think I am mad?' retorted Joe. 'No, no, strong no-trump.'

The Rabbi won the diamond lead with the ace and saw that he would need to set up dummy's club suit even if the king of hearts was onside. If a job had to be done, best to do it straight away. He led a club to the queen and East won with the king.

Now, thought the Rabbi, if a heart comes back I will rise with the ace and play another club. I can't afford the queen of hearts to lose to West's king. No, a diamond or a heart back would then kill it.

After some thought East in fact returned a diamond. His idea was to force the dummy, to kill the late trump entry to the club suit.

The Rabbi ruffed in the dummy, drew two rounds of trumps with the ace and queen, then led a second club towards the table. West rose with the ace and was on lead in this position:

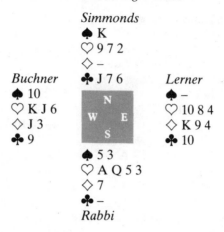

Simmonds
♠ K
♡ 9 7 2
◇ –
♣ J 7 6

Buchner
♠ 10
♡ K J 6
◇ J 3
♣ 9

Lerner
♠ –
♡ 10 8 4
◇ K 9 4
♣ 10

♠ 5 3
♡ A Q 5 3
◇ 7
♣ –
Rabbi

When West persisted with the jack of diamonds, the Rabbi discarded a heart from dummy. The defence was now at an end. If West played another diamond, the Rabbi would discard dummy's last losing heart and ruff in his hand; he could then play a trump to the king and enjoy dummy's clubs. West in fact switched to a heart but the Rabbi won with the queen and drew the last trump. When clubs proved to be 3–3 he was able to claim the contract.

'I see you're not telling him how to play *that* Four Spades!' exclaimed Joe Simmonds. He reached for the score-sheet. 'Well, this I find hard to believe. Three pairs not even in game.'

A round or two later the Rabbi had to check that his eyes were not playing tricks on him. He had just picked up this monster of a hand:

♠ A K 8 7 4 3   ♡ A K 7 5 4 2   ◇ 4   ♣ –

Partner surely had a fit for one of the suits but what could he open? Two Spades would be weak in their system and it didn't look right to open Two Clubs with only 14 points.

The Rabbi's speculations were cut short by Maureen Glickman, an elderly woman to his right. 'Five Clubs,' she said.

Ah well, she has made it easy for me, thought the Rabbi. 'Six Clubs.'

Joe replied Six Diamonds and the Rabbi continued to Six Hearts, offering a choice of the majors. There was no further bidding. West led the jack of clubs and this was the layout:

Game all
Dealer East

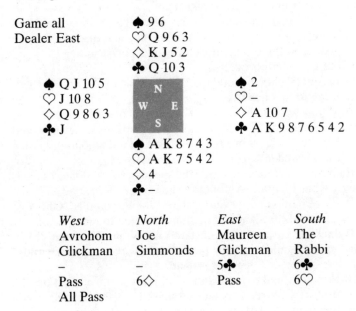

♠ 9 6
♡ Q 9 6 3
♢ K J 5 2
♣ Q 10 3

♠ Q J 10 5   ♠ 2
♡ J 10 8   ♡ –
♢ Q 9 8 6 3   ♢ A 10 7
♣ J   ♣ A K 9 8 7 6 5 4 2

♠ A K 8 7 4 3
♡ A K 7 5 4 2
♢ 4
♣ –

West	North	East	South
Avrohom	Joe	Maureen	The
Glickman	Simmonds	Glickman	Rabbi
–	–	5♣	6♣
Pass	6♢	Pass	6♡
All Pass			

The Rabbi paused to assess his prospects. Four trumps to the queen were good to see but after this vulnerable Five Club opening the breaks in the majors would be bad. What if he ruffed the club lead, drew one round of trumps to find them 3–0, then started to ruff spades? When he tried to return to his hand to take a second ruff he might suffer a trump promotion. Yes, it was quite likely that East held nine clubs.

An idea occurred to the Rabbi. 'Three of clubs, please,' he said.

East saw no reason to overtake and the Rabbi allowed West's jack of clubs to hold, discarding his singleton diamond. When West switched to the queen of spades the Rabbi won with the ace and cashed the ace of trumps, finding that the trumps were indeed

3–0. He continued with the king of spades, then ruffed a spade. Thanks to his careful manoeuvre at trick 1 he was now able to return to his hand with a diamond ruff. After a second spade ruff, establishing the suit, he cashed the bare queen of trumps and returned to his hand with a second diamond ruff to draw the outstanding trump. Twelve tricks made.

Avrohom Glickman smiled at his wife. 'The Rabbi found you asleep there,' he declared. 'Overtake the jack of clubs and he cannot discard the diamond. You would play another club and promote a trump for me.'

Maureen Glickman nodded. 'I did think of it,' she replied, continuing to nod her head.

'And you were right to reject the idea,' observed the Rabbi, coming to her aid. 'If you overtake I can ruff, draw trumps, and run the Q 10 of clubs through you to set up a diamond discard. I lose just one spade.'

Maureen Glickman increased the speed of her nodding. 'That is exactly what I feared, Avrohom,' she said.

'Well, this I don't believe,' declared Joe Simmonds. 'Only two other pairs bid the slam and neither managed to make it.'

'It does not surprise me,' declared Avrohom Glickman. 'Most players here would cover the jack of clubs with the queen without thinking. After that declarer is dead.'

Glickman turned to the Rabbi. 'Let me ask you a question,' he said. 'Before I retired I exhausted myself; I spent my whole life chasing money. Now it means nothing to me. We sit in the sun, we talk, we enjoy ourselves. Is it wrong to strive after wealth?'

'Money is a wonderful thing, Avrohom,' replied the Rabbi. 'But it's possible to pay too high a price for it.'

The final move of the evening brought Joe's wife, Katya, and her partner to the Rabbi's table.

'You and Joe are winning it?' asked Katya, taking the East seat.

The Rabbi smiled. 'If half a top above average is a winning score at this club, we are winning it,' he replied.

'The Rabbi has done his best,' Joe declared, 'but my over-bidding has defeated him.'

Katya Simmonds looked closely at her husband. 'When you play with me you do not overbid at all,' she said.

Joe measured his words carefully, 'The Rabbi is an honoured guest, Katya,' he replied. 'It is only polite to show confidence in his abilities.'

The Rabbi drew his cards for the penultimate board of the evening:

♠ K J 3   ♡ K 6 5   ◇ K 4 2   ♣ J 10 8 5

'One Spade,' said Katya Simmonds, to the Rabbi's right. Two passes followed and Joe protected with a double. Katya passed and the Rabbi considered his response. What should he say, 1NT or 2NT? Did Joe apply the notion of the 'borrowed king' when bidding in the protective seat? If so, 1NT would be enough. Still, that spade king–jack sitting over the opener looked as good as an ace–queen. 'Two No-trumps,' said the Rabbi.

Joe raised to 3NT and the queen of hearts was led. This was the complete deal:

East–West game
Dealer East

```
                    ♠ A 10 5 4
                    ♡ A 9 3
                    ◇ Q 8 3
                    ♣ Q 9 2
  ♠ 6                               ♠ Q 9 8 7 2
  ♡ Q J 10 8 2          N           ♡ 7 4
  ◇ 10 9 6 5       W        E        ◇ A J 7
  ♣ 7 6 3              S             ♣ A K 4
                    ♠ K J 3
                    ♡ K 6 5
                    ◇ K 4 2
                    ♣ J 10 8 5
```

West	North	East	South
Helen	Joe	Katya	The
Veldon	Simmonds	Simmonds	Rabbi
–	–	1♠	Pass
Pass	Dble	Pass	2NT
Pass	3NT	All Pass	

'I see what you mean by overbidding,' declared Katya, as the dummy appeared. 'How can you raise with only 12 points?'

'Are you forgetting the borrowed king?' replied Joe. 'You think the Rabbi will have a bare 11 for his jump to 2NT? With the borrowed king he will have more like 14.'

The Rabbi looked down at his three kings and two jacks. They were doing a very poor job of impersonating a 14-count. 'Small, please,' he said.

The queen of hearts was allowed to win and the Rabbi won the next round of hearts with dummy's ace. A finesse of the spade jack succeeded and the Rabbi continued with club to the 9 and king. Katya Simmonds exited safely with ace and another club, won in the dummy. When the Rabbi led a low diamond, East could not afford to rise with the ace. She played low and the Rabbi's king won the trick. He cashed the jack of clubs, throwing a heart from dummy, and surveyed this end position:

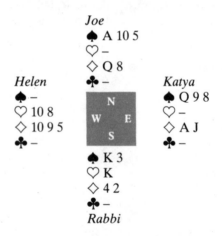

Joe
♠ A 10 5
♡ –
♢ Q 8
♣ –

Helen
♠ –
♡ 10 8
♢ 10 9 5
♣ –

Katya
♠ Q 9 8
♡ –
♢ A J
♣ –

♠ K 3
♡ K
♢ 4 2
♣ –
Rabbi

Confident how the cards lay, the Rabbi cashed the king of hearts, throwing a diamond from dummy. East had to retain her spade guard and therefore threw the jack of diamonds. The Rabbi now cashed the king of spades and exited with a diamond to the queen and ace. At trick 12 East had to return a spade into dummy's tenace and the game was made.

'You see?' exclaimed a delighted Joe. 'Did I not say he would have 14 points?'

'I made it only 11 points,' Katya replied.

'Yes, but he made it look like 14,' declared Joe triumphantly. 'The Rabbi may not borrow a king during the bidding. He borrows it during the play!'

The enjoyable evening drew to a close with this board:

Love all
Dealer West

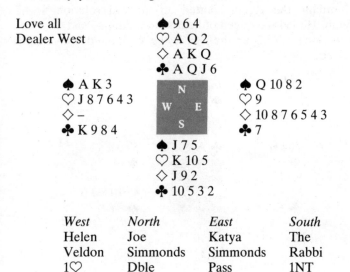

♠ 9 6 4
♡ A Q 2
◇ A K Q
♣ A Q J 6

♠ A K 3
♡ J 8 7 6 4 3
◇ –
♣ K 9 8 4

♠ Q 10 8 2
♡ 9
◇ 10 8 7 6 5 4 3
♣ 7

♠ J 7 5
♡ K 10 5
◇ J 9 2
♣ 10 5 3 2

West	North	East	South
Helen	Joe	Katya	The
Veldon	Simmonds	Simmonds	Rabbi
1♡	Dble	Pass	1NT
Pass	3NT	All Pass	

The ace of spades was led and Joe Simmonds caught the Rabbi's eye before displaying his dummy. 'I assume you show around a good 10-count for your 1NT response?' he enquired.

The Rabbi looked back uncertainly. 'Er . . . not necessarily quite so much,' he replied.

Simmonds laughed. 'No need to look so worried,' he said. 'I have 22 points for you.'

The Rabbi raised an appreciative eyebrow as the dummy appeared. The defenders cashed four spade tricks, the Rabbi discarding a club from his hand and, with the touch of a showman, the diamond ace from dummy. He won the heart return with dummy's ace and cashed the king and queen of diamonds.

The king of clubs was marked in the West hand but, even so, nine tricks were not guaranteed. If the Rabbi were to cash two more heart tricks, followed by the jack of diamonds, which club could he throw from the dummy? If he threw the 6, he would have to win the first round of clubs in the dummy and would not be able to repeat the club finesse. If instead he threw a club honour from dummy, West would cover a lead of the 10 from hand. What to do?

Eventually the Rabbi spotted an unusual solution to his problem. He led the queen of hearts from dummy and overtook with the king, setting up the jack in the West hand! These cards remained:

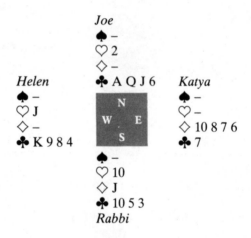

Joe
♠ –
♡ 2
♢ –
♣ A Q J 6

Helen
♠ –
♡ J
♢ –
♣ K 9 8 4

Katya
♠ –
♡ –
♢ 10 8 7 6
♣ 7

Rabbi
♠ –
♡ 10
♢ J
♣ 10 5 3

West had no good card to play on the diamond jack. If she discarded a heart, restoring declarer's third heart trick, the Rabbi would throw the low club from dummy, finesse once in clubs, then return to ♡10 to take a second club finesse. Helen Veldon in fact threw a club, but now the Rabbi discarded dummy's last heart and scored four club tricks by leading the 10.

'Values to spare, as I thought,' Joe declared. 'You could throw away an ace, overtake a queen with a king, and *still* make nine tricks!'

11.   Battle with the Arabs

The Rabbi spent the final week of his holiday in Jerusalem, with Marcia and George Bohm. On this particular evening the couple had a prior engagement.

'So bad I feel, leaving you like this,' said George Bohm. 'But my boss set up this dinner one month ago.'

'Some bosses would understand if we cancelled,' added his wife. 'Not Ishmael. George's career would be ended.'

'She exaggerates, of course,' said Bohm, searching for his car keys. 'Come, we must hurry. You know his attitude if people are late.'

Dressed in their finery, the Bohms departed. The Rabbi gazed out of the window of their fourth-floor apartment, admiring the lights of the city. What to do? It would be unthinkable back home, but . . . well, he had heard there was a high-stake game at the Jerusalem Hilton. Just a hand or two, to pass the time. Could that hurt anyone?

It was nine o'clock as the Rabbi stepped into the Hilton card-room. He winced at the clouds of smoke before him. What a habit! Several tables were in play but in the far corner he spotted a table with only three occupants, wealthy Arabs by all appearances. Perhaps they needed a fourth.

'May I join you?' asked the Rabbi.

The swarthy occupant of the corner seat blew out a cloud of smoke. 'This table is the 100 shekel game,' he replied. 'The 2 and 5 shekel games are over there.'

For a moment the Rabbi hesitated. How much was left of his funding for the trip? Around 1300 shekels, was it? Was there any law that he should lose a big rubber first time?

His heart pounding, the Rabbi nodded his acceptance of the stakes and took the vacant seat. The other three players wore desert costume of the finest quality. Their Rolex watches were no cheap imitations and their fingers glittered with gold and diamonds. 100 shekels was probably the amount they tipped for valet parking.

The first cut put the Rabbi in partnership with Khalid ben Zeid, a heavily-built man with a black beard. This was the opening deal:

Love all
Dealer South

```
                    ♠ Q J 4 3
                    ♡ A 6
                    ◇ A K 10 6
                    ♣ A 6 2
♠ A K 10 7 6                         ♠ 9 8 5 2
♡ J 10 5 3         N                 ♡ K
◇ 4             W     E              ◇ Q J 9 5 3
♣ J 10 7           S                 ♣ K 5 4
                    ♠ –
                    ♡ Q 9 8 7 4 2
                    ◇ 8 7 2
                    ♣ Q 9 8 3
```

West	North	East	South
The	*Sheikh*	*Khalid*	*Mahmoud*
Rabbi	*Nu'aimat*	*ben Zeid*	*Shura'ah*
–	–	–	Pass
Pass	1◇	Pass	1♡
1♠	2NT	Pass	3♡
Pass	3NT	Pass	4♡
All Pass			

Not overjoyed to find the opponents in game on the first hand, the Rabbi led the ace of spades. The balding Mahmoud Shura'ah ruffed in the South hand. He then played a trump to the ace, dropping the king from East. For a moment he paused to consider the implications of this. With two trump tricks to be lost he would need to find East with the king of clubs, maybe precisely king-to-three. He would also need to end-play West to avoid the loss of a diamond trick.

When a club was led from the table at trick 3 East played low, hoping that declarer had a guess in the suit. Shura'ah won with the queen and played a second club to the ace. Now, what was West's shape? Five spades, four hearts . . . he must have three clubs for the plan to work, so only one diamond! Shura'ah cashed the ace of diamonds, removing the Rabbi's holding in that suit, then played a third round of clubs to East's king. He ruffed the spade return and surveyed this end position:

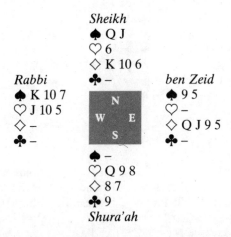

Sheikh
♠ Q J
♡ 6
♢ K 10 6
♣ —

Rabbi
♠ K 10 7
♡ J 10 5
♢ —
♣ —

ben Zeid
♠ 9 5
♡ —
♢ Q J 9 5
♣ —

♠ —
♡ Q 9 8
♢ 8 7
♣ 9
Shura'ah

Mahmoud Shura'ah now led the 9 of trumps from his hand. The Rabbi won with the 10 and had no good return. A trump would allow declarer to draw trumps, then score a club and a diamond. When he chose instead to return the king of spades, South ruffed with the 8. He drew another round of trumps with the queen, throwing a diamond from dummy, then led his master club. The Rabbi could make one more trump trick but that was all. The game had been made.

The Rabbi did not know what had impressed him more, declarer's immaculate card play or the fact that no-one had thought it worthy of comment. It seemed that he had stepped into a game of the highest standard. He would need to play well himself, or . . . it was best not to think of the consequences.

At the worst possible moment the Rabbi's ability to pick up big hands seemed to have deserted him. It was Mahmoud Shura'ah who had a chance to win the first rubber.

North–South game   ♠ A K 9 2
Dealer North   ♡ 8
                          ◇ 10 9 5 4 2
                          ♣ A K 7

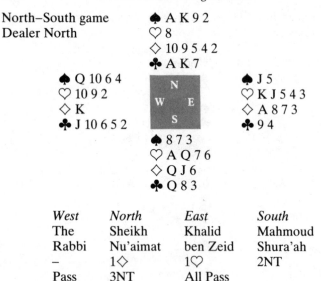

♠ Q 10 6 4   ♠ J 5
♡ 10 9 2   ♡ K J 5 4 3
◇ K   ◇ A 8 7 3
♣ J 10 6 5 2   ♣ 9 4

                          ♠ 8 7 3
                          ♡ A Q 7 6
                          ◇ Q J 6
                          ♣ Q 8 3

West	*North*	*East*	*South*
The	Sheikh	Khalid	Mahmoud
Rabbi	Nu'aimat	ben Zeid	Shura'ah
–	1◇	1♡	2NT
Pass	3NT	All Pass	

The Rabbi led ♡10 and this card was allowed to hold. He
continued with ♡9, somewhat surprised to see this card win the
trick too. Declarer won the third round of hearts and led the
diamond queen. The Rabbi captured this with the bare king but
had no heart to play. Declarer was able to establish three tricks in
the diamond suit, bringing his total to nine.

The North player, a born leader of men if ever there was one,
looked across at his partner. 'If the Jew switches to a spade?' he
said.

Shura'ah turned to the Rabbi. 'You had four spades?'

The Rabbi nodded.

'No good then,' declared Shura'ah. 'He can clear a spade trick
when he wins the diamond king but Khalid then has no spades.'

The Rabbi did not dare to tot up the first rubber. He sat with his
eyes half closed, waiting to hear his fate.

'Eleven hundred,' announced Khalid ben Zeid.

The Rabbi opened his eyes. So, by a small margin he was still
solvent! He reached for his wallet and handed over the requisite
sheaf of blanknotes.

'Another rubber?' enquired Mahmoud Shura'ah.

For a moment the Rabbi hesitated. If he lost the next rubber and could not pay up, what fate would befall him? Ah well, think positively, they say. 'Another rubber, yes,' he replied.

This time the cut put the Rabbi in partnership with Mahmoud Shura'ah. As the Rabbi was dealing the cards, his partner caught his eye. 'Tell me one thing,' he said. 'You Jews have suffered for century after century. How can you still have optimism for the future?'

'It has to do with relative gratitude,' replied the Rabbi. 'If a Jew breaks his leg, he gives thanks that he did not break both legs. If he breaks both legs, he gives thanks that he did not break his neck. We always give thanks because we know things could be worse, usually much worse.'

For example, thought the Rabbi, it would be very much worse to lose two rubbers than just one.

This was the first deal of the new rubber:

Love all
Dealer South

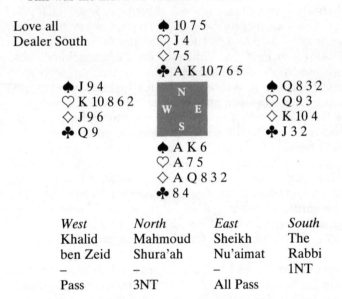

```
                    ♠ 10 7 5
                    ♡ J 4
                    ◇ 7 5
                    ♣ A K 10 7 6 5
♠ J 9 4                              ♠ Q 8 3 2
♡ K 10 8 6 2         N               ♡ Q 9 3
◇ J 9 6          W       E           ◇ K 10 4
♣ Q 9               S               ♣ J 3 2
                    ♠ A K 6
                    ♡ A 7 5
                    ◇ A Q 8 3 2
                    ♣ 8 4
```

West	North	East	South
Khalid	Mahmoud	Sheikh	The
ben Zeid	Shura'ah	Nu'aimat	Rabbi
–	–	–	1NT
Pass	3NT	All Pass	

Khalid ben Zeid led ♡6 against 3NT. The Rabbi tried dummy's jack and allowed East's queen to win the trick. He ducked the ♡9 continuation and won the third round of hearts with the ace, throwing a spade from dummy. The best idea now was surely a club to the 10, thought the Rabbi. The safe hand would be on lead and if the clubs divided 3–2 he would have nine tricks.

When the Rabbi led a low club towards dummy, Khalid ben Zeid was quick to insert the queen. They defend well, thought the Rabbi, as he reached for dummy's ace of clubs. Not that he would expect anything less at these exalted stakes.

If West had started with ♣Q J x, a finesse would bring in the suit. Still, honour doubleton was more likely. Also, West might have put in the queen from Q x x, in which case the jack would drop from East. What to do? If the club suit would not oblige there was still the chance of scoring four diamonds. Yes, and in that case an avoidance play would be needed; he would have to lead diamonds twice towards the South hand, to prevent East unblocking the king from K x x.

At trick 5 the Rabbi led a diamond from dummy. Since he had not yet abandoned hope in the club suit, he rose with the diamond ace. A club to dummy's king failed to drop the jack and the Rabbi continued with another diamond. East played low and the queen won the trick. A third round of diamonds drew the jack from West and the king from East. The Rabbi won the spade return and faced his remaining cards, claiming nine tricks.

Sheikh Nu'aimat, in the East seat, turned his black eyes towards the Rabbi. 'For a Jew you play well,' he observed.

The Rabbi met his eyes. 'For an Arab, your partner defends well,' he replied. 'The queen of clubs was a good card.'

Sheikh Nu'aimat nodded. 'On the five-shekel table you would not meet such a defence,' he replied.

With an imperious flick of the finger the Sheikh summoned a hotel servant, demanding fresh charcoal for his hookah pipe. He then turned once more towards the Rabbi. 'You would be offended if I told an Arab joke?' he said.

'What, me?' replied the Rabbi. 'I have probably heard it already.'

'A very old Arab is on his deathbed,' recounted the Sheikh. 'To the surprise of his wife, many children and even more grand-children, he calls for a Rabbi, saying he wants to become a Jew.'

The Rabbi leaned forward, listening politely.

'So, the Rabbi arrives,' continued the Sheikh, 'and asks him why he wants to become a Jew after living all his life as a good Moslem. You know what the Arab replies?'

The Rabbi shook his head.

'Better one of them should die than one of us!'

The Rabbi smiled. 'Very good,' he said.

'You have heard it before?'

'Well, one a little similar,' replied the Rabbi mischievously. 'I forget it exactly. It was something about an elderly Jew on his deathbed.'

The Sheikh's hookah pipe was soon restored to action and play continued. All did not go the Rabbi's way and the score reached Game All. Then, a chance of salvation. The Rabbi arrived in a slam.

Game all
Dealer South

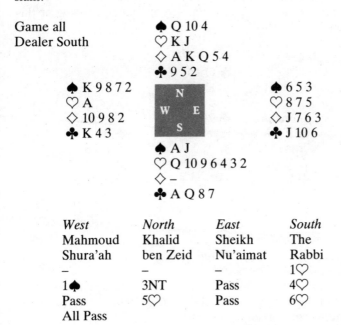

	♠ Q 10 4	
	♡ K J	
	◇ A K Q 5 4	
	♣ 9 5 2	
♠ K 9 8 7 2		♠ 6 5 3
♡ A		♡ 8 7 5
◇ 10 9 8 2		◇ J 7 6 3
♣ K 4 3		♣ J 10 6
	♠ A J	
	♡ Q 10 9 6 4 3 2	
	◇ –	
	♣ A Q 8 7	

West	*North*	*East*	*South*
Mahmoud	Khalid	Sheikh	The
Shura'ah	ben Zeid	Nu'aimat	Rabbi
–	–	–	1♡
1♠	3NT	Pass	4♡
Pass	5♡	Pass	6♡
All Pass			

West led ◇10 and the Rabbi gazed in disappointment at the dummy laid out for him. So much in diamonds opposite his void! After the vulnerable overcall from West both black kings were likely to be offside. What could be done?

It seemed to the Rabbi that he would need to find West with a singleton ace of trumps, in which case he could be end-played. First West's diamonds must be removed. How many would he hold? If only three, the play would be diamond ace and king, throwing two clubs to preserve both the black-suit tenaces. He could then ruff a diamond and exit in trumps, eventually reaching dummy with a trump to cash the other diamond honour.

The Rabbi won the opening lead with the ace of diamonds and immediately cashed the king. He threw two clubs from hand, East meanwhile following with the 7 and 3, suggesting an even number of diamonds. The Rabbi was inclined to believe the signal. Yes, he was going to play for the diamonds to be 4–4.

The Rabbi cashed the queen of diamonds, discarding the spade jack. He then ruffed a diamond in his hand, pleased to see both defenders follow. He cashed the ace of spades, arriving at this position:

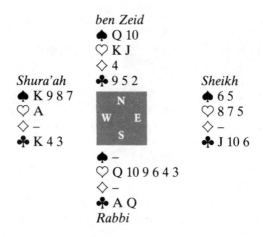

ben Zeid
♠ Q 10
♡ K J
♢ 4
♣ 9 5 2

Shura'ah
♠ K 9 8 7
♡ A
♢ –
♣ K 4 3

Sheikh
♠ 6 5
♡ 8 7 5
♢ –
♣ J 10 6

♠ –
♡ Q 10 9 6 4 3
♢ –
♣ A Q
Rabbi

A trump to the ace left West end-played. Muttering a prayer of some sort, he flipped a small club onto the table. 'Twelve tricks,' said the Rabbi, spreading his cards.

'*Anwar befaq'hasset!*' exclaimed the Sheikh, throwing the hookah pipe to one side. '*Meir z'habla en qu'hajh isse baqah-baqah ain infaq'hasset fa a'iloqah!*'

The Rabbi's partner leaned forward. 'Sheikh Nu'aimat suggest that possibly good idea if trump ace is led.'

The Rabbi nodded. 'Not a good idea as far as we would be concerned,' he replied.

Still peering furiously at his partner, the Sheikh produced a well-filled wallet. '*En fassan m'hat, pardah qa'hen wahah'walla!*' he cried, tossing some notes in the Rabbi's direction.

The Sheikh's partner was not one to take criticism lightly. He rose threateningly to his feet, a Yemeni dagger at his belt.

'Gentlemen, please,' declared the Rabbi. 'Are you not forgetting the rules? I believe Arabs are meant to fight Jews, not other Arabs.'

Still eyeing each other intently, the two Arabs resumed their seats. The Rabbi was mightily relieved as he stocked his wallet with the proceeds from the second rubber. Suppose he had lost and been unable to pay? He could imagine the headlines back home, perhaps even on the front page of the *News of the World*. 'Rabbi Hacked to Death in High-stake Card Game.' What would his congregation have thought?

The next rubber saw the Rabbi and Sheikh Nu'aimat in partnership.

Love all
Dealer North

```
                     ♠ 10 7 4
                     ♡ 4 2
                     ◇ J 8 4
                     ♣ A K 10 3 2
  ♠ 9 6 3                              ♠ 8
  ♡ K 10 8 3          N                ♡ Q J 7 5
  ◇ K 5 3          W     E             ◇ 9 7 6 2
  ♣ J 7 4             S                ♣ Q 9 8 5
                     ♠ A K Q J 5 2
                     ♡ A 9 6
                     ◇ A Q 10
                     ♣ 6
```

West	North	East	South
Mahmoud	Sheikh	Khalid	The
Shura'ah	Nu'aimat	ben Zeid	Rabbi
–	Pass	Pass	2♣
Pass	3♣	Pass	3♠
Pass	4♠	Pass	6♠
All Pass			

No flicker of displeasure came to the face of Mahmoud Shura'ah as the opponents reached a slam. Much of his adult life had been spent playing high-stake bridge and he accepted the good and the bad as it came to him. He led a low heart against Six Spades, his partner's jack forcing declarer's ace. The Rabbi played the ace of trumps, noting the appearance of East's 8.

What now? A heart ruff would bump the total to eleven but he would still need a successful diamond finesse. So many shekels to risk on a finesse. How about setting up the clubs? Yes, that must be better.

The Rabbi cashed ♣A K successfully, throwing a heart. He then ruffed a club with the king, both defenders following. Two further entries to dummy were needed in the trump suit. Was East's ♠8 a singleton or had he started with ♠9 8? The holdings were roughly equal in probability but from the doubleton might not East at least some of the time have played the 9?

The Rabbi led ♠2 from his hand and finessed dummy's 7. It was a joyful moment as East paused for a moment, then discarded a diamond. The Rabbi ruffed a club with the queen and returned to dummy with a trump to the 10. He discarded his last heart on the thirteenth club and ran the jack of diamonds. The finesse lost to the king but he was able to claim the remainder, making twelve tricks.

Sheikh Nu'aimat puffed contentedly on his hookah, the smoke bubbling through the water. He eyed the Rabbi respectfully. 'Restricted Choice in the trump suit?' he queried.

The Rabbi nodded.' You would be sympathetic if I had lost to 9 8 doubleton?' he said.

'It would be as Allah wished it,' replied the Sheikh.

'Tell me,' asked Mahmoud Shura'ah. 'Why do you Jews always answer one question with another question?'

The Rabbi considered this for a moment. 'Why not?' he replied.

The cards were soon redealt and the Rabbi gazed in disbelief at this hand.

♠ A K 5 2   ♡ A K 6   ◇ –   ♣ A K Q J 10 6

Already one game ahead, with the stakes set at an unimaginable 100 shekels. Then . . . he picks up a hand like this! Was this some dream induced by the hookah smoke?

'Three no-trumps,' said Khalid ben Zeid, to the Rabbi's right. This was a Gambling 3NT, indicating a solid minor suit.

So much for any learned investigation of the prospects, thought the Rabbi. Should he simply blast the grand in clubs? Best not to be greedy in this world. 'Six Clubs,' said the Rabbi.

'Six Diamonds,' said Mahmood Shura'ah, to the Rabbi's left.

The call ran back to the Rabbi. What to do now? A double would pick up around 800, minus whatever honours the opponents could claim. Surely his fine hand was worth more than that. Was there any law prohibiting partner from having some spades in his hand? 'Six Spades,' said the Rabbi.

There was no further bidding. West led ♢8 and the Rabbi awaited the dummy with some apprehension.

North–South game   ♠ J 8 3
Dealer East   ♡ Q 7 2
                   ♢ 9 7 5 4 3
                   ♣ 7 3

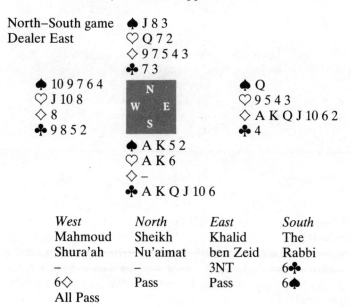

♠ 10 9 7 6 4   ♠ Q
♡ J 10 8   ♡ 9 5 4 3
♢ 8   ♢ A K Q J 10 6 2
♣ 9 8 5 2   ♣ 4

                   ♠ A K 5 2
                   ♡ A K 6
                   ♢ –
                   ♣ A K Q J 10 6

West	North	East	South
Mahmoud	Sheikh	Khalid	The
Shura'ah	Nu'aimat	ben Zeid	Rabbi
–	–	3NT	6♣
6♢	Pass	Pass	6♠
All Pass			

The Rabbi winced at the disappointing trump holding in dummy. Three to the jack? Three to the queen would probably have been good enough. Provided the trumps were no worse than 4–2 he could have ruffed the opening lead, drawn three rounds of trumps, and simply run his winners. West would ruff in at some stage but would then have no diamond to return.

What chance was there? Ah yes, East might hold queen double-ton of trumps. Then the same play would work. The Rabbi ruffed the diamond lead and cashed the ace of trumps. The queen duly appeared from East. Unfortunately, one trick too early. So, thought the Rabbi, West has five trumps. The penalty they could have taken from Six Diamonds was beginning to look more attractive by the moment.

The Rabbi was not prepared to give up. When he led a low trump from his hand, West split his 10 9 and dummy's jack won the trick. Four rounds of clubs came next, West following all the way. The Rabbi cashed the ♡A and K, leaving these cards still to be played:

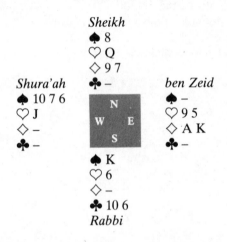

Sheikh
♠ 8
♡ Q
♢ 9 7
♣ —

Shura'ah
♠ 10 7 6
♡ J
♢ —
♣ —

ben Zeid
♠ —
♡ 9 5
♢ A K
♣ —

♠ K
♡ 6
♢ —
♣ 10 6
Rabbi

A heart to the queen was followed by a diamond from dummy, ruffed with the king. Mahmoud Shura'ah had to underruff on this trick and the Rabbi continued with a club from hand. Dummy's 8 of trumps was promoted, *en passant*, and the slam had been made.

Sheikh Nu'aimat could hardly believe what he had seen. 'The Jew made it?' he gasped.

The Rabbi sat back triumphantly as the opponents settled for the rubber. What a night it had been! The most exciting of his life. With over 4000 shekels in his wallet it was time to leave. Quit while you are ahead. Yes, that was the rule.

Mahmoud Shura'ah gathered in the cards and subjected them to a fierce riffle shuffle. 'Another rubber?' he said.

For just a moment the Rabbi paused. 'Why not?' he replied.